Date Due

HISTORY OF IDEAS SERIES

No. 4

THE HISTORY OF IDEAS SERIES

Under the editorial sponsorship and direction of the Editorial Committee, *The Journal of the History of Ideas*: John Herman Randall, Jr., chairman, George Boas, Gilbert Chinard, Paul O. Kristeller, Arthur O. Lovejoy, Marjorie H. Nicolson, Philip P. Wiener

Other volumes in preparation

TOLSTOY
AND CHINA

by Derk Bodde

WITH THE COLLABORATION OF

GALIA SPESHNEFF BODDE

PRINCETON

PRINCETON UNIVERSITY PRESS

1950

891.72
T58zb

PREFACE

THIS study originated from a chance remark by my wife, Galia Speshneff Bodde, to the effect that she had once vaguely heard of the existence of a bust of the Chinese philosopher, Lao Tzu, in Tolstoy's study at Yasnaya Polyana. Though resulting investigation has revealed no trace of this bust, it has brought to light abundant evidence of Tolstoy's interest in China, most of which, to my knowledge, has never heretofore been presented. For the collecting of this evidence I owe a deep debt of gratitude to my wife. She it was who carefully examined the voluminous Russian sources and translated the pertinent data into English; without her painstaking work this book could never have been written.

All dates here given are in "old style" (i.e., for the nineteenth century, twelve days behind the Gregorian calendar), save for the events occurring outside of Russia which are mentioned on pp. 44-45. Chinese names, which often appear with confusing variations in different sources, are all romanized according to the Wade-Giles system, unless they occur spelled otherwise in the titles of books. Russian names are transcribed according to the system found in Ernest J. Simmons' *Leo Tolstoy* (item 5 in the Bibliography at the end of this book).

The fact that many of the most important Russian sources are unavailable in Philadelphia, where most of the research for this monograph has been conducted, has made its preparation a task of more than usual difficulty. Compensation has been provided, however, by the cooperation of several persons, to whom I am happy to express my hearty thanks. Mr. Elliott H. Morse and his colleagues, of the Reference Department, University of Pennsylvania Library, kindly arranged for the interlibrary loan of numerous books from the Library of Congress and Harvard University. Mr. Avrahm Yarmolinsky, Chief of the Slavonic Division, New York Public Library, unfailingly answered several queries on bibliographical matters. Similar aid was given by Mr. Sergei Polevoy, of the Harvard-Yenching Institute, Cambridge, Mass., who has taken a personal interest in this study, he himself being the author of an unpublished study (in Russian) of the influence of Tolstoy in China. (The present study is devoted wholly to the influence of China on Tolstoy.) Further bibliographical information was supplied by Professor Ernest J. Simmons, Chairman of the Department of Slavic Languages, Columbia University; Mr. Fang Chao-ying, of the Chinese History Project, Columbia University; Mr. Constantine Kiriloff of Peiping; and Mr. Joseph Wang, of the Asiatic Division, Library of Congress. The help of other kind friends on specific points is acknowledged in the footnotes.

To the board of editors of the History of Ideas Monograph Series, especially Dr. Arthur O. Lovejoy, Professor Emeritus of Philosophy, The Johns Hopkins University, I am deeply grateful for including this book among their monographs. I am likewise indebted to Mr. Owen Lattimore, Director of the Walter Hines Page School of International Relations, The Johns Hopkins University, for first bringing me in contact with Professor Lovejoy.

DERK BODDE
Associate Professor of Chinese
University of Pennsylvania

October 1, 1949
Philadelphia, Pa.

CONTENTS

TOLSTOY AND CHINA

CHAPTER I

CHINA, THE WEST, AND TOLSTOY

AMONG the countries of the Orient with which the Western world has at various times come in contact, China, though farthest removed, has seemed peculiarly capable of inspiring either ardent admiration or violent antipathy. As early as the thirteenth century, the fascination that Cathay then exercised upon Europeans is obvious to all who have read Marco Polo. Less well known, except to specialists, is the equally strong enthusiasm that held sway in several of the countries of Western Europe during much of the seventeenth and eighteenth centuries. In France, where this enthusiasm was highest, it is probable that during the first three quarters of the eighteenth century the cultural influence of China was more potent than that of any other non-European country.

Much of this Sinomania was as ephemeral and superficial as it was intense. Already strong in the seventeenth century, it became further stimulated in the eighteenth by that search for the exotic and the fanciful which generally characterized the rococo age, and was given impetus by the growing influx into Europe of such new Chinese products as tea, silk, porcelain, and lacquer ware. In the field of art it left its mark in the charming *chinoiseries* of the time. In the more purely intellectual sphere, however, the *goût chinois* was equally manifest and perhaps of more enduring significance. The Jesuit missionaries who then lived in Peking—some even as officials at the Chinese court—wrote lengthy accounts to their *confrères* at home, filled with admiration for the strange civilization they saw. These, published in Latin or French and often translated into other languages, left a deep impression upon some of the leading minds of the age.

Leibniz, for example, was inspired by them in 1697 to suggest that, just as European missionaries were being sent to China, so Chinese missionaries should be induced to come to Europe as bearers of oriental culture. The result, so he hoped, would be a blending of East and West into a sort of intellectual "one world."[1] Seventy years later François Quesnay, leader of the Physiocrats, published a book, *Le despotisme de la Chine* (1767), in which, using Jesuit sources, he painted a glowing picture of Chinese political and economic institutions to support his own theories.[2] At about the same time Voltaire, who was a life-long admirer of China, wrote in his *Dictionnaire philosophique* (1764): "One need not be obsessed with the merits of the Chinese to recognize that the organization of their empire is in truth the best that the world has ever seen."[3]

This enthusiasm, however, died abruptly with the French Revolution, and during the nineteenth century came to be replaced by an attitude that was all too often actively contemptuous when it was not passively indifferent. In Western writings of this century on China, such epithets as "dirty," "cruel," "corrupt," "decadent" and "heathen" occur only too frequently. Many causes can be adduced for

[1] An excellent recent study of Leibniz's interest in China is that of Donald F. Lach, "Leibniz and China," *Journal of the History of Ideas*, vol. 6 (1945), pp. 436-455.

[2] A translation of this book, accompanied by an analysis of Quesnay's indebtedness to China, has been made by Lewis A. Maverick, *China a Model for Europe*, Paul Anderson Co. (San Antonio, Texas, 1946).

[3] *Oeuvres complètes* (Gotha ed. of 1785), xxxviii, 492; quoted in Adolph Reichwein, *China and Europe* (New York, 1925), p. 89.

this, surely one of the most startling reversals of opinion in the history of thought.[4] Primary, no doubt, were the rise of industrialism, nationalism and imperialism in the West— movements which unhappily coincided with a rapid decline of the Manchu ruling power in China, accompanied by internal economic and cultural decay.

Western interest in China did not cease as a result of these developments, but it shifted its emphasis from the purely intellectual sphere to the more practical concerns of the diplomat, businessman and proselytizing missionary. The literature on China that flowed from the pens of such men proves by its very abundance that it must have reached a considerable public. Its net effect upon intellectual circles, however, was incomparably less than that of the Jesuit writings of a century earlier.[5] There is no doubt that the famous lines of Tennyson:

> "Better fifty years of Europe,
> Than a cycle of Cathay,"

accurately reflect the attitude of most people of his day.

In France, more than elsewhere, the old intellectual interest survived to some extent, to find expression in the writings of a small group of serious scholars and literary men. Even there, however, it was diluted by a romanticism which increasingly turned to the more colorful but also more superficial aspects of a "quaint" Japan.[6] Indeed,

---

[4] Several are suggested by Reichwein, *op. cit.*, pp. 149-153, and Mary Gertrude Mason, *Western Concepts of China and the Chinese, 1840-1876*, Columbia University Ph.D. Thesis (New York, 1939), pp. 252-263.

[5] See the excellent study by Mason cited above.

[6] See William Leonard Schwartz, *The Imaginative Interpretation of the Far East in Modern French Literature, 1800-1925*, Honoré Champion (Paris, 1927).

among the outstanding Western thinkers of the nineteenth century, Emerson was one of the very few who displayed a respectful, if not too ardent, interest in the ideological side of Chinese civilization.[7]

It is against this prevailing background that we should study the attitude towards China of Leo Tolstoy (1828-1910). His knowledge and appreciation of Chinese civilization, and especially of Chinese philosophy and religion, was, if not wholly objective, certainly deep and sincere. Among all the intellectual figures of the nineteenth century, in fact, there was probably none, outside of the narrow circle of sinologists and others whose lives were linked with China through personal circumstances, who read as widely and intensively on that country as did Tolstoy.

This interest in China came as a direct result of Tolstoy's religious "crisis," which, beginning in the second half of the 1870's, caused him to turn away from a fruitful literary career and devote his remaining years to a search for the religious meaning of life and death; it was not long before this search led him to China and her sages. In the rich literary output of his first fifty years, therefore, only a few scattered references can be found that indicate any awareness of China, and these, though sympathetic in tone, reveal the characteristic misconceptions of his time.[8]

[7] Arthur Christy, *The Orient in American Transcendentalism: A Study of Emerson, Thoreau, and Alcott*, Columbia University Press (New York, 1932), esp. pp. 123-137, 317-321.

[8] In 1862 Tolstoy wrote: "I involuntarily recall the Chinese war, in which three great Powers quite sincerely introduced the belief of progress into China by means of powder and cannon-balls." Cf. *Progress and the Definition of Education*, W 4.168 (= Leo Wiener's English translation of the works of Tolstoy, vol. 4, p. 168; on this and other important sources used for the present study, see the Bibliography). Tolstoy is here referring to the hostilities of 1856-60, through

In the years immediately following the "crisis," Tolstoy —in addition to Christianity itself—at first confined himself to the study of Buddhism and Islam.[9] Only in 1882 did his intellectual horizons expand to include the Far East, as shown by passing reference to Confucius in two letters.[10] In the latter part of 1883, however, and more especially in 1884, his serious study of China and Chinese thought began, and was to continue, intermittently but intensively, until his death in 1910.

Thus Tolstoy's interest in China should be viewed within the larger context of a ceaseless quest for religious and moral understanding, which sent him to the nineteenth-century American social and religious writers on the one hand, and to the wisdom of the ancient Hindus, Persians, Arabs, Jews, Greeks and Romans on the other—as well as, of course, to European thought itself. Yet within this

---

which the major Western participants, Britain and France (as well as Russia and the United States; one wonders what Tolstoy means by the "*three* great Powers"), gained important political and economic concessions in China. Other sympathetic references to China's role in this war appear in the same essay (p. 164) and in *Lucerne* (1857; W 3.256-257, 259). In 1862 Tolstoy wrote approvingly of the Chinese as the only people who, recognizing the fallacy of the idea of "progress," had deliberately restricted the use of printing. See his *On Popular Education* (W 4.20-21). In so writing he betrays his ignorance of the fact that China is the original home of printing, and that there, as in no other country, the written and printed word has for centuries been regarded with almost superstitious reverence. The same concept of China as a country that has rejected progress appears elswhere in this essay (p. 6), and even more strikingly in *Progress and the Definition of Education* (W 4.162).

[9] All three religions are mentioned in *My Confession* (1879; W 6.57), in which, however, there is no reference to China.

[10] Letter 116 to N. N. Strakhov of June 8 (?), 1882 (JE 63.98), and letter to W. A. Engelgardt of December 20 (?), 1882 (*ibid.*, p. 117). (JE 63.98 = Jubilee Edition in Russian of Tolstoy's works, vol. 63, p. 98, on which see below and Bibliography.)

truly world-wide search, it is remarkable how warmly and frequently Tolstoy's feeling for China and her philosophers expresses itself, the more so as it was only in his last five years that he had the opportunity of entering into personal contact with Chinese intellectuals. This fact justifies the verdict uttered by Romain Rolland in 1928: "Of them all [the Asiatic civilizations which Tolstoy studied], it was China whose thought was closest to him. And yet it was she who gave herself up to him the least. From 1884 onward he studied Confucius and Lao Tzu; the latter was his favorite among the sages of antiquity. But, in actual fact, Tolstoy had to wait until 1895 in order to exchange his first letter with a compatriot of Lao Tzu."[11]

Three studies have so far appeared on the subject of Tolstoy's contacts with Asiatic civilizations: Birukoff, Paul [Biryukov, P. I.], *Tolstoi und der Orient, Briefe und sonstige Zeugnisse über Tolstois Beziehungen zu den Vertretern orientalischer Religionen*, Rotapfel-Verlag (Zürich & Leipzig, 1925) (hereafter referred to as Biryukov); Rolland, Romain, "La réponse de l'Asie à Tolstoy," *Europe, Revue Mensuelle*, Paris, no. 67 (July 15, 1928), pp. 338-360; and Shahani, Ranjee G., "Hinduism in Tolstoy," *Asiatic Review*, London, n.s. vol. 28 (1932), pp. 664-669.[12]

Of these three studies, that by Biryukov, one of Tolstoy's most devoted disciples, is by far the most valuable. It includes an impressive bibliography of Tolstoy's readings on Asia, in addition to chapters on his contacts with Hindus, Muslims, Japanese and Chinese, and on his own writings

[11] Rolland, p. 340 of article cited immediately below. The date of 1895 is a mistake for 1905.

[12] For another possibly forthcoming study in Russian on Tolstoy and China, see Appendix A.

regarding the Orient. Several of the latter, quoted *in extenso* in German translation, have not, until recently, been elsewhere available. In scholarship, however, Biryukov's monograph leaves much to be desired. Documentation is sometimes inexact, and names of persons and books are frequently incomplete or misspelled; some, indeed, appear differently in different parts of the book. Furthermore, Biryukov's evident unfamiliarity with the civilizations of Asia forces him to reduce to a minimum any critical evaluation of his data.

Little need be said of Rolland's article, since it is largely based on Biryukov's work. Though the same is not true of Shahani's article, the latter is rendered almost valueless by its chauvinistic attempt to trace most of Tolstoy's ideas to Indian sources, largely on the presumption of an ethnic link asserted by the author to exist beteween Russians and Asiatics. Typical of its point of view is the statement on p. 669 (unsupported by any factual evidence): "The fact is ignored that the Christianity of the Russian sage derives directly from Hinduism; and it passes without recognition that what seems to Western Europeans a new message is in a new guise the thought of India."

The present study differs from those preceding it inasmuch as it confines itself wholly to Tolstoy's relations with China; its approach is that of a person whose primary field is Chinese philosophy. Before drawing any conclusions as to how Tolstoy's thinking might have been affected by his interest in China, it tries to present the concrete evidence necessary to prove that this interest was an actual fact. This could never have been done without recourse to extensive sources in Russian (diaries, notebooks, correspondence, etc.) which were either disregarded by the authors of the previous three studies, or had not yet been published when these men wrote. Particularly indispensable has been the monumental Soviet definitive edition of Tolstoy's works, known as the Jubilee Edition. Though only 39 of the 95 volumes planned for this edition have appeared since the beginning of publication in 1928, these fortunately contain much of the material that is essential for our purpose; furthermore, their detailed editorial notes give many pertinent excerpts from forthcoming volumes.[13]

[13] On this work (cited in the present study as JE) and on the other chief sources used, with their abbreviations, see the Bibliography.

CHAPTER II

TOLSTOY'S READINGS ON CHINA

I N HIS *Tolstoi und der Orient*, pp. 258-263, Biryukov lists 54 books, pamphlets and periodicals, relative to various oriental civilizations, religions and philosophies, which he says existed in Tolstoy's library at Yasnaya Polyana. Thirteen of them are important for our purpose because they relate directly to China. These can be more than doubled, however, by examination of other sources, particularly Tolstoy's diaries and correspondence, in which numerous additional publications on China are mentioned as having reached Tolstoy in the form of loans, gifts or purchases. The result is a total of 32 publications on China (some mere pamphlets, others works in as many as three volumes) which can be stated with assurance to have passed through Tolstoy's hands at one time or another. There are, in addition, seven "uncertain items," here so designated either because they cannot be precisely identified, or because, though referred to in correspondence between Tolstoy and others, it is not definitely ascertainable whether they actually reached him or not.

In Appendix B of the present book will be found a detailed list of all these works, arranged, when the data permit, according to the years in which they first reached Tolstoy's attention, or, when this is impossible, according to their dates of original publication. They are grouped under the following categories: I. General and Miscellaneous (nos. 1-10); II. Confucianism (nos. 11-18); III. Taoism (nos. 19-28); IV. Buddhism (nos. 29-32); V. Uncertain Items (nos. 33-39).

That this list is not exhaustive is strongly suggested by some of Tolstoy's own writings.[1] As it stands, however, it gives us a clear picture of his predominantly philosophical and religious interest in China, being wholly confined, aside from the general and miscellaneous works (several sent as gifts by admirers), to the three major philosophies or religions of China: Confucianism, Taoism and Buddhism (especially the two former).

Even within these fields, furthermore, the list shows certain limitations. In the section on Confucianism, for example, the "Four Books" (which comprise the philosophical core of that system) are all represented by at least two translations, whereas of the "Five Classics" (which though also a part of the Confucian canon, are less exclusively philosophical), only two are included.[2] The same selectivity is found in the section on Taoism: almost all of its items are devoted to the famous *Tao Te Ching* of Lao Tzu (traditionally a sixth century B.C. elder contemporary of Confucius, but today regarded by most critical scholars as belonging to the fourth or third century); other Taoist thinkers, on the other hand, notably Chuang Tzu (ca. 369-ca. 286 B.C.), are largely disregarded. This is hardly surprising, as in Tolstoy's day the terse classic of Lao Tzu was incomparably better known to the West than Chuang Tzu's longer work, even though the latter in many ways represents the culmination of early Taoism.[3]

---

[1] See below, pp. 26, 41, 88.

[2] These are the *Shih Ching* or *Book of Odes* (vol. 3 in item 12) and the *Shu Ching* or *Book of History* (included in item 18). The "Four Books" are the *Confucian Analects* (sayings of Confucius), *Works of Mencius, Great Learning* and *Doctrine of the Mean*; direct translations of them are contained in items 12-13, 16-18 and 37, while they are also touched upon in several of the other items.

[3] Partial translations of the *Chuang-tzu*, however, are contained in

Once this is granted, however, it is remarkable to what extent Tolstoy's readings include, within their self-chosen limitations, the really significant products of the sinology of his day. The list in our Appendix includes the works of British, American, French, Belgian, German, Austrian, Russian, Chinese and Japanese authors or translators, written in English, French, German and Russian. Specialists on China will recognize in it the names of many of the most familiar nineteenth century writers on that country: such men as T. T. Meadows, James Legge, Samuel Beal, Lafcadio Hearn, Paul Carus, M. G. Pauthier, Stanislas Julien, Eugène Simon, Léon de Rosny, Charles de Harlez, Ernest Faber, Victor von Strauss, V. P. Vasilyev, Ku Hung-ming and Liang Ch'i-ch'ao.

In using the works of these men, furthermore, Tolstoy on the whole shows excellent discrimination. Thus in the case of Confucianism, it is above all Legge's *Chinese Classics* (item 12) which he repeatedly cites with appreciation; this monumental work, despite many successors, still remains the standard translation of these texts today. The same is true of Lao Tzu's *Tao Te Ching*: from his first acquaintance with this philosopher in 1884, until 1893, Tolstoy seems to have depended primarily on the early but excellent translation of Julien (item 19).[4] The many other translations which he subsequently acquired include such

items 22-23, and it is somewhat surprising that Tolstoy seems never to have commented on this, one of the most brilliant works in all Chinese literature.

[4] In 1893 Tolstoy commented on this work: "The best translation [of Lao Tzu] . . . is that by Stanislas Julien." See *"The Non-Acting"* (W 23.49). See also Tolstoy's defense of Julien to Stasov, cited on p. 26 below.

first-rate ones as those of Legge (item 23) and Carus
(item 27).

It is scarcely surprising that Tolstoy's readings are
heavily weighted in favor of European sinology, since in
his day few Chinese or Japanese scholars were yet writing
in Western languages, and American sinology was still in
its infancy. There is at least one American work, however,
which would probably have interested Tolstoy had he been
aware of its existence. It is S. Wells Williams' *The Middle
Kingdom*, a book which still retains considerable value
even today.[5]

Among Tolstoy's general readings on China, two deserve
special mention, both because of their intrinsic importance
and because, having been read by Tolstoy in his early years
of Chinese interest (1884 and 1887 respectively), they
presumably played an important part in shaping his concepts of China. They are the first two items on our list:
T. T. Meadows' *The Chinese and Their Rebellions* (1856)
and Eugène Simon's *La cité chinoise* (1885).

Meadows, who died in 1869 after long service as a British diplomatic officer in China from 1842 onward (at first
as interpreter in Canton and then as Consul), was one of
the most enlightened and philosophically minded Westerners to write on China during the nineteenth century. His
book—much broader in scope than its main title indicates—
remains even now a remarkable account of Confucianism
as the basis of Chinese society and government.

Of the Chinese political institutions favorably noted by
Meadows, none struck him more forcibly than the govern-

[5] S. Wells Williams, *The Middle Kingdom, a Survey of the Geog-
raphy, Government, Literature, Social Life, Arts, and History of the
Chinese Empire*, 2 vols., Wiley & Putnam (New York and London,
1848; last revised ed., 1883).

mental examination system, through which all classes of society, with trifling exceptions, were permitted to compete for public office in periodic examinations based upon a knowledge of the Chinese classics. This system impressed itself upon Meadows as the key fact explaining the long continuity of Chinese civilization. Indeed, a primary purpose of his book (as well as of an earlier one of 1847) was to persuade his fellow countrymen to adopt a similar system for the British Empire. In this attempt he was eminently successful, for a recent study has not only demonstrated the primary role of Chinese influence in the instituting of Britain's civil service system in the mid-nineteenth century, but also the importance of Meadows' books as transmitters of this influence.[6]

Meadows' general attitude toward China is well exemplified by the following excerpt (*op. cit.*, pp. 384-385): "The Chinese nation, with a written history extending as far back as that of any other the world has known, is the only one that has throughout retained its nationality, and has never been ousted from the land where it first appeared. And that it has, between civil wars like the present—wars necessary for the production of beneficial changes, whether administerial or dynastic—enjoyed long periods of a safety to life and property, even now scarcely exceeded in the most civilized countries in the West, is a truth as well known from authentic history, as it may be inferred from the fact that its numbers now equal half of the rest of the human race, while its industrial products penetrate into every region of the earth. It is surprising what a large

[6] Teng Ssu-yü, "Chinese Influence on the Western Examination System," *Harvard Journal of Asiatic Studies*, vol. 7 (1943), pp. 267-312, esp. 267, 289-290.

number of occidentals can manage *not* to see the sufficiently plain inference, that results, so long enduring and so vast, must be owing to the social and political life of the Chinese being founded on great and eternal truths. . . . There is one class of the stolid that requires special mention. . . . The grand characteristic of the man of this class lies in his greeting everything that he never heard of, or never saw before, either with solemn brays of reprobation or broad grins of derision. . . . Even to the stolid man himself, I may however make it dimly comprehensible, that in some branches of the social sciences it is just possible that the Chinese may be in advance of the West, in spite of their shaving their heads and wearing tails—aye, and dreadful thought! shoes with white soles to them."

This book, one of the nineteenth-century works best calculated to give Tolstoy an intelligent and at the same time favorable picture of Chinese civilization, elicited from him his warm approval: "I have read Meadows' work on China. He is entirely devoted to the Chinese civilization, like every sensible, sincere man who knows Chinese life. In nothing is the significance of ridicule seen better than in the case of China. When a man is unable to understand a thing, he ridicules it. China, a country of 360 millions of inhabitants, the richest, most ancient, happy, peaceful nation, lives by certain principles. We have ridiculed these principles, and it seems to us that we have settled China."[7]

[7] W 19.184. This utterance is placed by Wiener, Tolstoy's English translator, under a section entitled *Thoughts and Aphorisms*, sub-sect. *Varia*; the latter he dates as March, 1887. This date, however, seems doubtful for this particular passage, because, as we know from another source (Gusev, p. 316), Tolstoy read Meadows on July 9-13, 1884, which would therefore be the logical time for him to make such a comment. Wiener's ignorance of Meadows' identity is also shown by the

Simon's *La cité chinoise*, the other general work on China read by Tolstoy in his early years of Chinese interest, is in its own way equally remarkable. Though almost totally forgotten today, it was once a best seller, as shown by the fact that it passed through no less than seven French editions between 1885 and 1891, in addition to being translated into Russian (1886, the version read by Tolstoy), English (1887),[8] and, as late as 1920, German.[9] We know of its author (who died in 1896) that he spent some ten years in China, at first (1860-64) in the study of Chinese agriculture on behalf of the French Ministry of Agriculture, and then as French Consul in various cities. From his own words he appears to have been one of the most widely traveled Westerners of his time in China; his itinerary carried him from Canton in the south to Mongolia in the north, as well as far into the interior of the country.[10]

Simon's book is essentially sociological. Its chapters on "the family," "labor," "the state," etc., contain abundant statistical data, and it concludes with a detailed "case study" of a prosperous farm in South China. In title and plan it may well have been inspired by Fustel de Coulanges' fa-

---

fact that he transcribes his name into English as "Médov." That Tolstoy was actually referring to Meadows, however, is proved by his remarks on ridicule, which derive from the passage in Meadows just quoted, as well as by his Chinese population figure of 360 million, which is that given in Meadows' book, p. 1.

[8] Entitled *China: Its Social, Political, and Religious Life*, Low, Marsten, Searle & Rivington (London, 1887). Citations below are from this English edition.

[9] Paul Garin, transl., *Das Paradis der Arbeit; ein Weg in eine deutsche Zukunft* (*La cité chinoise*), J. C. Huber (Diessen vor München, 1920).

[10] Simon, *op. cit.*, pp. 8, 22; Henri Cordier, "Nécrologie," *T'oung Pao*, Leyden, vol. 7 (1896), pp. 592-593.

mous similar analysis of classical society, *La cité antique* (1864).[11]

Simon's approach to his subject, however, is such as to make his book a major curiosity of nineteenth-century sinology. The value of its detailed factual material, much of it based on accurate personal observation, is constantly marred by such an extreme bias in favor of everything Chinese as can be equaled only in the more colorful seventeenth- and eighteenth-century Jesuit accounts. The net effect is particularly startling against the generally somber opinions of Simon's contemporaries. The following passages give a glimpse of this curious mélange of the factual and fantastic: "I can state that in Hankow, a town in which I lived for some time, only one murder took place in thirty-four years. . . . I wish also I could enable the reader to see them [the Chinese peasants] at their meals, sufficient in quantity, and composed of much more varied materials than those forming the subsistance of our field labourers. . . . Especially should I like to enable him to compare the light, frank and easy bearing of the first Chinese peasant he might meet with the heavy, overburdened, awkward and shamefaced demeanour of most of our small agriculturists. . . . Their very appearance shows that there exists between rich and poor, or rather the less well-to-do—between the countrymen and townsmen—much less distance and difference than among ourselves" (pp. 7-8).

These passages, though undeniably overdrawn, contain a modicum of truth and do credit to their author's capacity for sympathetic approach toward an alien civilization in an age when such capacity was far from common among

---

[11] This has been suggested to me by Professor J. J. L. Duyvendak, Director of the Sinologisch Instituut, University of Leyden.

Westerners. The following statements, however, definitely overstep the bounds of reality and enter the freer realm of fancy:

"There is scarcely a single Chinese who is unable to read, write, cast accounts, and draw" (p. 17).

"Speaking as one who passed ten years in China, and travelled through the country from north to south, and east to west, I can declare that I have never known a case of infanticide" (p. 22).

"Nowhere do there exist so few beggars as in China. There are certainly many in Pekin whose importunities are most distressing; but they are far below the 400,000 assisted poor of Paris" (p. 23).

No wonder that Tolstoy, on reading this book, wrote with the highest enthusiasm to Biryukov in November, 1887: "Novosyolov also brought me the book of Simon (in Russian translation) about China. Without fail, get it and read it. This reading simply delighted me, and to you, in particular, it will be very useful and heartening because he describes agriculture in it, as well as the whole life of the Chinese. Here is a book that should and must be rendered for 'Posrednik.' "[12]

But though the books of Meadows and Simon served supremely well to give Tolstoy a sympathetic view of China, they actually merely stimulated an interest that had already been aroused by his study of Chinese philosophy. This becomes clear if we turn to examine Tolstoy's readings on China as a whole.

[12] JE 86.145 n5. "Posrednik" is the name of the publishing firm organized by Tolstoy and his followers to make worthwhile literature available to the masses. See beginning of ch. 3. For the results of Tolstoy's suggestion, see pp. 34-35.

The chronological arrangement of these readings indicates four periods in which his interest in China reached a peak: those of 1884, 1893, 1900, and 1909-10. This interest, which seems to have begun at the end of 1883, is first explicitly stated in a letter he wrote to V. G. Chertkov, his closest friend and follower, in the latter part of February, 1884: "I sit at home with fever and a severe cold in the head, and read Confucius for the second day. It is difficult to realize its extraordinary moral height. One delights in seeing how this teaching at times approaches the height of the Christian teaching."[13]

From the early part of 1884 until July 9-13 of the same year (when Tolstoy read the book of Meadows), numerous letters and diary entries testify to his intense preoccupation with this new field of interest.[14] Thus on March 4-6 he wrote to Chertkov: "I am occupied with Chinese religion. I have found much that is good, useful and heartening for myself. I want to share it with others, God willing" (JE 85.33). And again on March 11: "I am very much occupied with Chinese wisdom. I should greatly like to tell you and everybody else of that moral good which these books have done me" (JE 85.37).

The books in question not only included the Confucian "Four Books," in Legge's translation, but also Lao Tzu's *Tao Te Ching*, in the translation of Julien. On March 6 Tolstoy wrote in his diary: "Have been translating Lao

[13] JE 85.30, 31 n1. That Tolstoy's reading on China and Chinese thought must have begun some time before this letter was written is shown by the references to Chinese religion which appear in *My Religion* (W 16.104, 106-107, 125-126, 130, 184-185), the finishing touches to which were made by Tolstoy in January, 1884. Two of these are quoted below on pp. 65 and 87.

[14] JE 54.436 n149; Gusev, pp. 304-306, 308, 316.

[20]

Tzu. Does not come out as I want" (JE 25.883). Another entry of March 23 reflects his preoccupation with both Confucianism and Taoism: "Remarkable indeed is Confucius' *Doctrine of the Mean*. In it, as with Lao Tzu, the fulfillment of natural law is what constitutes wisdom, strength and life. And this law fulfills itself silently, its meaning unrevealed. It is the *Tao*, which unfolds itself evenly, imperceptibly and without trace, and yet has powerful effect.[15] I do not know what will result from my preoccupation with the teaching of Confucius, but it has already brought me much good. Its characteristic is truth, oneness, and not doubleness. He says that Heaven always acts genuinely."[16]

In the years following 1884, references in Tolstoy's diary and letters, as well as quotations of Confucian and Taoist sayings in his published writings, give abundant evidence of his continuing interest in "Chinese wisdom."[17] In the latter months of 1893 this interest flared into a second period of major preoccupation, and on November 5 of that year he wrote to Chertkov as follows: "I have been rereading Lao Tzu and now have begun reading Legge, the volume containing Mo Ti. I should like to write a book

[15] This sentence is reminiscent of the *Tao Te Ching*, chs. 21 and 25. The *Tao* (Way, Road, Path) is the name given by the Taoists to that metaphysical and impersonal first principle from which all things in the universe derive their being.

[16] JE 54.436 n150; Biryukov, p. 12. The last sentence is an echo of what is said in the *Doctrine of the Mean*, ch. 26. Only the first sentence is quoted in passing in the JE citation, the volume of which containing the complete text of Tolstoy's diary for 1884 still awaits publication.

[17] A partial list follows: *1885*: April-May 15 (?) (JE 63.318); *1886*: Feb. 14 (W 17.171), June 1 (JE 63.362), July 15-16 (JE 85.370), August (W 19.155); *1888*: Feb. 7 and 17 (JE 86.117-118, 120 n4, 124; these are all on Chinese Buddhism); also W 16.244, 283; *1889*: March 12 (JE 86.218, 221 n3); *1892*: August (W 19.115-116), September (W 19.80-81).

about Chinese wisdom, and particularly a discussion about human nature being good, and human nature being evil, and that people must be either egoistic individualists, or must be loving. All this is very interesting and important to me, and I should like to make it accessible to all and to write about it.

"Please send me, if you do not need them, the remaining books of Legge and Pauthier, provided you have them" (JE 87.236).

Tolstoy is here referring to the second volume of Legge's *Chinese Classics*, on Mencius (ca. 371-ca. 289 B.C.), the most famous follower of Confucius, who is chiefly noted for his doctrine of the innate goodness of human nature, and who had many arguments with philosophical opponents on this subject. Regarding Mo Ti, we shall have more to say presently. By Pauthier, Tolstoy means the partial translation of Lao Tzu by that scholar which is listed in Appendix B as item 25.

On November 12 Tolstoy wrote again to Chertkov on this subject: "I wrote you about the Chinese, asking you to send me Legge and Pauthier, and wanted to do this work. But now it is clear to me that it should be done by you, and that you will do it easily and beautifully. The work consists of translating Legge's two volumes on Confucius and Mencius [*Chinese Classics*, vols. 1-2], with all his [Legge's] investigations into the lives of these sages and of the philosophers contemporaneous and close to them. (I do not remember about the book of Confucius, but in Mencius there is an account of these philosophers, among them Mo Ti, which is extremely interesting as well as important.) Mencius himself is also exceptionally interesting. If you could manage an introduction for this book (it must be written as a single book: *Chinese Sages*), that would be fine. But if not, then simply a translation of Legge—omitting only some of the overly dogmatic Christian remarks—would be one of the best books for the intellectual 'Posrednik.' Firstly, because for most of the reading public all this is completely new; secondly, the subjects discussed are the most important ones in the world and are treated with seriousness; and thirdly, many highly moral ideas are beautifully expressed. So as soon as you tell me that you agree, I shall send you all I have. As for Buddha, finish it up.[18] You have made an excellent beginning and should not dig too deeply with the plow. *Le mieux est l'ennemi du bien*" (JE 87.239).

On November 24 Tolstoy wrote to Chertkov yet a third time: "I still want to look through the books on Chinese wisdom in order to work out a plan more clearly. As soon as I finish this one of these days, I shall send them to you. A marvellous work. . . ." (JE 87.242). The project, however, like that on the Buddha, was left undone by Chertkov. At this point the reader may wonder why Tolstoy, in his enthusiasm, did not carry it out himself. The reason, no doubt, is that this same period saw him busily engaged on quite a different Chinese project: the preparation, in collaboration with E. I. Popov, another of his followers, of a new Russian translation of Lao Tzu. For this purpose he now supplemented Julien's French translation, on which he had hitherto largely depended, with other later versions,

[18] This was a popular account of the life and teaching of Buddha, concerning which Tolstoy had already corresponded with Chertkov on February 7 and 17, 1888 (JE 86.118, 120 n4, 124). It was, however, never completed by Chertkov (JE 87.242 n5).

particularly the German translation of Victor von Strauss (1870).[19]

In preparation for his task, Tolstoy wrote to the well known writer, N. S. Leskov, early in October, 1893, requesting the names of St. Petersburg sinologists to whom he (Tolstoy) might apply for authoritative information about Lao Tzu.[20] During October and November of the same year he also engaged in a lengthy correspondence on the same subject with V. V. Stasov, librarian of the Imperial Public Library in St. Petersburg. The latter, as a consequence, made many inquiries among the sinologists of the capital on Tolstoy's behalf. At the same time he collected book reviews of several Lao Tzu translations. In a lengthy letter of October 24 he reported unfavorably on the earlier translations of Julien, Chalmers, Rémusat and Plaenckner, while calling Tolstoy's attention to the more recent versions by Harlez, Rosny and Balfour.[21] On Strauss, however, his verdict was particularly unfavorable.[22]

Tolstoy promptly replied with a vigorous defense of Julien as a man of "very careful scholarship (he follows Chinese commentaries)." At the same time, however, he requested further information about Strauss, whose translation obviously interested him deeply.[23] Stasov's reply of November 6 was unequivocal and (as any scholar of Chinese will agree today) entirely correct: "The Professor of Chinese in our University, [A.O.] Ivanovski, says that Strauss is a *third-rate* sinologist and that he cannot be trusted."[24] In the same letter he recommended Legge's

[19] JE 87.224 n2. The Strauss translation is item 21 in Appendix B.
[20] Gusev, p. 485.
[21] Respectively items 19-20, 35-36, 22, 24 and 34 in Appendix B.
[22] *Stasov*, pp. 102-106.   [23] *Ibid.*, p. 109.   [24] *Ibid.*, p. 112.

recent translation of the *Tao Te Ching* (item 23). As a result of this and further correspondence until the end of the year, it and the translations of Chalmers and Harlez were sent to Tolstoy.[25]

Undaunted by Stasov's adverse reports, Tolstoy continued working on his translation until the middle of May, 1894,[26] apparently using Strauss as a basis. The result was never printed, however, and is promised for initial publication in the forthcoming thirty-first volume of the Jubilee Edition.[27]

Tolstoy's next period of intensified preoccupation with Chinese thought came in the last three months of 1900. Conceivably it may have been inspired to some extent by events connected with the Boxer Rebellion in China of the summer of that year, on which more will be said in the following chapter. This time Tolstoy seems to have concerned himself almost wholly with Confucianism. On October 5 he wrote in his diary: "Reading Chinese classics. Very important . . ." (JE 54.45). Again on November 12: "Feeling fine. Writing nothing, but studying Confucius, and everything's fine. Derive spiritual strength" (JE 54.54). And yet again two days later: "Studying Confucius and all the rest is insignificant. Seems good. What is most important is that this teaching, which tells one to be particularly watchful over oneself, when alone, has a powerful and beneficial effect on me. If only I could keep it in its freshness."[28]

[25] *Ibid.*, pp. 115-116, 118, 120.   [26] Gusev, p. 498.
[27] See JE 87.224 n2. Yet one wonders if this unpublished version may not have been the basis for the Tolstoy pamphlet on Lao Tzu of 1910 (see p. 32 below, item 6).
[28] JE 54.62. The statement about self-watchfulness refers to a sentence in the *Great Learning*, ch. 6: "The superior man must be watch-

During these last months of 1900 Tolstoy is also said to have received "a whole pile of English books about China" from the Rumyantzev Museum in Moscow.[29] However, of the works identified in our list in Appendix B as having come to his attention in 1900 (items 3-6, 38-39), only F. Max Müller's *Religions of China* (item 6) is in English. This is one of several indications that this list of Tolstoy's readings on China is incomplete.

Until now we have been concerned largely with the story of Tolstoy's study of Lao Tzu and the Confucian classics. Yet there is another thinker, lying outside these major schools, in whom he also felt a deep interest, though this fact is not immediately apparent from his list of readings. This is the philosopher Mo Ti, whose name has already appeared in Tolstoy's letters of November 5 and 12, 1893 (quoted on pp. 21-22 above). Mo Ti, better known in China as Mo Tzu,[30] is believed to have lived approximately 479-381 B.C., i.e., midway between Confucius (551-479) and Confucius' major follower, Mencius (ca. 371-ca. 289). He founded a school of thought, known after him as that of the Mohists, which for several centuries was the major rival of Confucianism (at that time far from being the unquestioned orthodoxy it became later). Curiously enough, however, the Mohists completely disappeared as

---

ful over himself when he is alone." Tolstoy alludes to it again under date of November 19 (JE 54.63). Other quotations by Tolstoy from Confucian writings appear during this same period in his diary of December 8 (JE 54.70) and in a letter of ca. December 23 (JE 72.538).

[29] JE 54.448 n181.

[30] Mo is his surname; Ti his personal name. The word Tzu, suffixed to the names of many Chinese philosophers (Mo Tzu, Lao Tzu, etc.), simply means "Master" (i.e., the Master Mo, the Master Lao, etc.). Western writings on Mo Tzu often refer to him as Mi Ti or Mih Ti.

an organized school by the second century B.C., leaving almost no trace on later Chinese thought.

This school shows striking superficial resemblances to Christianity in its vigorous condemnation of aggressive warfare, its prime insistence upon the need for all men to love one another equally if world peace is to be attained, and its assertion that the reason why men should do so is that there exists a supreme divine being who wills it thus. The Mohists further resemble the more puritanical sects of Christianity in their uncompromising insistence upon the truth of their own ideas, the rigid discipline which the leaders of the school exacted from their followers, and their ascetic denial of all luxury and of such cultural pursuits as music. Their arguments against these last, however, also reveal a basic difference between Mohist and Christian thought. Luxury and music are attacked on pragmatic rather than moral grounds : they are the economically unproductive manifestations of a leisure class; hence they should be made subordinate to the more basic physical needs of the population as a whole. Such utilitarianism, rather than moral judgment, is used by the Mohists as the final touchstone for evaluating all activities: war is condemned primarily because it is economically and socially wasteful, and only secondarily because it is morally wrong ; universal love is upheld primarily because it brings well-being to all men, and only secondarily because it is morally admirable in itself.

Despite this pragmatic basis, one may readily see how several of these ideas agree with Tolstoy's own pacifism, Christian love, asceticism, and opposition to the corrupting influences of human civilization in its more sophisticated aspects. In the nineteenth century Mo Tzu was but little known to the West,[31] and might never have come to Tolstoy's attention at all were it not for the fact that the views of the Chinese philosopher are the object of a strong attack from Mencius. Legge, as a consequence, devotes a section (pp. 103-125) in the prolegomena of his second volume of *The Chinese Classics* to a brief account of the Mohist philosophy; in this he translates Mo's famous essay on universal love.

Tolstoy seems first to have commented on this essay in a letter to Chertkov dated March 15, 1890: "A very good work awaits someone who knows English and understands the meaning of Christ's teaching. It is this: In the Chinese books in English—I have forgotten the translator—which I had and which you now have, there is Mo Ti's doctrine of love. Do you remember? In the teachings of Mencius and Confucius (especially Mencius) there is a refutation of this doctrine. Well, then, to translate all this and prepare a book, to show that this doctrine of love—as an extremely utilitarian doctrine—had been presented so long ago among the Chinese, and that it had been very poorly refuted, and that this doctrine—an earthly, utilitarian one, without the idea of a Father, or, most important, of *life*, i.e., eternal life—had a great influence. This would be excellent" (JE 87.19).

We have seen how Tolstoy later reverted to this idea, especially in his letter to Chertkov of November 12, 1893,

[31] There were, however, at least two works available on Mo Tzu: Ernst Faber's *Die Grundgedanken des alten chinesischen Socialismus oder die Lehre des Philosophen Micius*, Trübner (London, 1877), and Alexandra David's *Socialisme chinois, le philosoph Meh-ti et l'idée de solidarité*, Luzac (London, 1907), but Tolstoy seems not to have been acquainted with either. The best translation in English today is Y. P. Mei, *The Ethical and Political Works of Motse*, Arthur Probsthain (London, 1929).

and we shall see in the next chapter what finally resulted. Tolstoy's continuing awareness of Mo Tzu is evinced on several occasions in the years following 1893.[32]

Tolstoy's readings on China continued to the end of his life, reaching a final peak in 1909-10. On May 4 and August 15, 18 and 24 of the former year, we know that he was reading Confucius, Mencius and Lao Tzu.[33] This reading, as we shall see in the following chapter, was connected with the preparation of several pamphlets on China then in progress under Tolstoy's direction. On April 17, 1910, a copy was sent to him from Shanghai of *The World's Chinese Students' Journal*, published by "the progressive Chinese youth in English."[34] In his diary he commented that this "interests me very much"; as proof of this statement he also penciled marginal notes to one of its articles, "The Civilization of China." At the same time he is reported to have remarked: "Were I young, I would go to China."[35] These words, uttered in his eighty-second year, were followed less than six months later by his death on November 8, 1910.

[32] February, 1902, in *What Is Religion?* (W 24.124); letter of December 4, 1905 (see below p. 48); and references in Gusev (pp. 737, 816, 761) under April 28, August 15 and December 2, 1909.

[33] Gusev, pp. 738, 816, 751.   [34] See Appendix B, item 10.

[35] JE 58.39, 364 n555.

CHAPTER III

TOLSTOY'S WRITINGS AND PUBLICATIONS
ON CHINA

IT IS obvious that intellectual curiosity alone—keen
though this always was for Tolstoy—is not enough to
explain his interest in "Chinese wisdom." Rather it
was its spiritual content which seized him—so powerfully,
indeed, that he felt irresistibly compelled to make it widely
known to the public at large. The reader may remember the
words he wrote to Chertkov on March 4-6, 1884, when first
immersed in Chinese thought: "I have found much that is
good, useful and heartening for myself. I want to share it
with others, God willing."[1]

The instrument for carrying out this wish was a new
publishing organ, known as "Posrednik" or "The Intermediary," which Tolstoy created in this same year in conjunction with Chertkov and I. D. Sytin, an important Moscow publisher. Its purpose was to bring to the masses, in
cheap illustrated booklets, stories and philosophical and
religious writings culled from world literature by Tolstoy and his associates (Chertkov, Biryukov, P. A. Boulanger, etc.), and rewritten in a simple Russian style. Original compositions by Tolstoy were included as well. This
enterprise, which continued until Tolstoy's death, proved
to be one of the most worthwhile of all his ventures. "In
the first four years of its existence the little *Intermediary*
booklets, priced at one and one-half kopeks, sold twelve
million copies."[2]

[1] See above p. 20.
[2] Ernest J. Simmons, *Leo Tolstoy* (Boston, 1946), p. 393.

The following is a list of all those writings and publications on China with which Tolstoy was in one way or another associated. Some are "Posrednik" booklets (apparently not available in this country) which were prepared either by Tolstoy himself or by his followers under his direction. Others are Tolstoy's own writings, of which some have never been published until recently in the Jubilee Edition, or are scheduled for future publication in that work.

LIST OF TOLSTOY'S WRITINGS
AND SPONSORED PUBLICATIONS ON CHINA[3]

1884 1. Tolstoy, *Chinese Wisdom* (Kitaiskaya mudrost)[4]

1889 2. *How the Chinese Live* (Kak zhivut kitaitsy), from the book of G. Eugène Simon, "Posrednik" (Moscow, 1889)

1900 3. Tolstoy, *Epistle to the Chinese* (Poslaniye k kitaitsam) ; also known as *Christians to the Chinese People* (Khristiane k kitaiskomu narodu)[5]

1904 4. Boulanger, P. A., *The Life and Teaching of Confucius* (Zhizn i ucheniye Konfutsiya), with an essay by

---

[3] For much of the bibliographical data that follow, P. E. Skachkov's *Bibliografiya Kitaya* (Moscow-Leningrad, 1932) has been invaluable. In addition to the items below, there is an article, "Le mensonge chinois," signed "Léon Tolstoï," which appeared in *La Revue et Revue des Revues*, Paris, vol. 35 (fourth trimester, 1900), pp. 34-39. Henri Cordier, *Bibliotheca Sinica*, vol. 4 (Paris, 1907-08), col. 2583, lists the article with the comment: "This article has been translated into German, English and Russian." But then he adds: "It would not seem to be actually by Tolstoï." In this he is undoubtedly correct, for though the subject matter of the article (the evil effects of industrialism and other aspects of Western civilization upon Chinese social life) is consonant with Tolstoy's ideology, its lurid presentation and undistinguished style clearly reveal the hand of an inferior imitator.

[4] Unfinished fragment, published for the first time in JE 25.532-535, according to editor's statement in *ibid.*, p. 883. But see also below, item 5.

[5] Unfinished fragment, the sketches of which are to be published in the forthcoming JE vol. 34.

Tolstoy, "Chinese Teachings" ("Kitaiskoye ucheniye"), "Posrednik" (Moscow, 1904)[6]

1907 5. Tolstoy, *1. Letter to a Chinese; 2. Chinese Wisdom: the Thoughts of Chinese Thinkers* (1. Pismo k kitaitsu; 2. Kitaiskaya mudrost: mysli kitaiskikh myslitelei), "Posrednik" (Moscow, 1907), pp. 43[7]

1910 6. *The Sayings of the Chinese Sage Lao-tzu* (Izrecheniya kitaiskovo mudretsa Laotze), selected by Tolstoy, with an essay by I. Gorbunov-Posadov, "About the Sage Lao-tzu" ("O mudretse Laotze"), and an essay by Tolstoy, "On the Essence of Lao-tzu's Teaching" ("O suschnosti ucheniya Laotze"), "Posrednik" (Moscow, 1910), pp. 16[8]

1910 7. Boulanger, P. A., *Confucius, His Life and Teaching* (Konfutsi. Zhizn yevo i ucheniye), edited by Tolstoy, "Posrednik" (Moscow, 1910), pp. 47 (2nd ed., 1911, pp. 32)[9]

1910 8. Boulanger, P. A., *Remarkable Thinkers of All Times and Peoples. Mo Ti, a Chinese Philosopher: the Doctrine of Universal Love* (Zamechatelnyie mysliteli vsekh

---

[6] The JE editors seem to be mistaken when they date this as 1903 (JE 54.436 n149; 85.31 n1). The date of 1904 (confirmed in Skachkov, *Bibliografiya Kitaya*, p. 434) is given in JE 25.883. A revised version of this was published in 1910. See item 7.

[7] The *Letter* was originally published in German in *Die Neue Freie Presse* (November 1906) and in French in the *Courrier Européen* (November-December 1906); it was then translated from French into Russian in the newspaper, *Novoye Vremya* (New Age), no. 11026 (November 21, 1906). See JE 36.695-696. It is now available in *ibid.*, pp. 290-299, and in Biryukov, pp. 130-142. As for *Chinese Wisdom*, one wonders if it is the same as item 1 of 1884 above, despite the statement of the JE editors (see under this item) that the latter has been published for the first time only in the JE.

[8] This actually appeared on November 24, 1909 (Gusev, p. 761), though the title page bears the date of 1910. Tolstoy refers in his diary to the correction of the preface on August 23, 1909, and to the correction of the proofs on September 5 and 7-9 (*ibid.*, pp. 816, 752).

[9] Tolstoy writes in his diary of correcting the proofs of this on September 29-30 and November 21-22, 1909 (Gusev, pp. 754, 758); it appeared in print on March 11, 1910 (*ibid.*, p. 768). It is apparently a revision of item 4 above.

vremyon i narodov. Miti, kitaiski filosof: ucheniye o vseobshchei lyubvi), edited by Tolstoy, "Posrednik" (Moscow, 1910), pp. 16 (2nd ed., 1911, pp. 32)[10]

1911 9. Tolstoy, *1. A Surat Café (from the French)* ; *2. The Chinese Sage Lao-tzu* (1. Surratskaya kofeinaya [s frantsuzkovo] ; 2. Kitaiski mudrets Laotze), no. 15 of the Library of L. N. Tolstoy, edited by P. I. Biryukov, I. D. Sytin Co. (Moscow, 1911), pp. 32[11]

1913 10. Konishi, D. P., *Lao-tzu, Tao-te-ching: or the Scripture of Morality* (Lao-si, Tao-te-king: ili pisaniye o nravstvennosti), edited by Tolstoy, with a note by S. N. Durylin (Moscow, 1913), pp. 72

In addition to the foregoing, all directly concerned with China, Tolstoy compiled several other works of more general scope, in which, however, many sayings from Chinese wisdom find a prominent place :[12]

Thoughts of Wise People for Every Day (Mysli mudrykh lyudei na kazhdy den), "Posrednik" (Moscow, 1903)[13]
Circle of Reading (Krug chteniya), 2 vols., "Posrednik" (Moscow, 1906)[14]
For Every Day (Na kazhdy den), St. Petersburg, 1909-10[15]
The Pathway of Life (Put zhizni), "Posrednik" (Moscow, 1911)[16]

All these latter books consist of moral and religious sayings, collected by Tolstoy from world literature as well as from his own writings, and usually grouped under various

[10] Tolstoy writes in his diary of correcting the proofs of this on December 2, 1909 (Gusev, p. 761) ; it appeared in print on April 28, 1910 (*ibid.*, p. 773).

[11] The first part of this has nothing to do with China, as Surat is a city in India near Bombay. Whether or not the second part, on Lao Tzu, is the same as item 6 above is uncertain.

[12] See for these esp. JE 85.31 n1, 222 n6, 372 n6.

[13] To be published in JE vol. 39.

[14] To be published in JE vols. 40-42.   [15] Published in JE vols. 43-44.

[16] To be published in JE vol. 45. English translation by Archibald J. Wolfe, *The Pathway of Life*, 2 vols., International Book Publishing Co. (New York, 1919).

categories. The *Circle of Reading,* for example, contains thirty-one major themes, entitled "Faith," "The Soul," "One Soul in All," "God," "Love," etc. Often Tolstoy freely modified the sense of the quotations collected by him to suit his own purpose, so that it is difficult to identify them precisely with their originals.[17]

Of these compilations, with which Tolstoy became increasingly preoccupied in later years, the *Circle of Reading* has the longest history, its inception going back to 1884. Thus on March 15 of that year he wrote in his diary: "I ascribe my good moral state of mind to the reading of Confucius and Lao Tzu. I must arrange for myself a *Circle of Reading:* Epictetus, Marcus Aurelius, Lao Tzu, Buddha, Pascal, and the Evangelists. This would also be essential for everybody else" (JE 85.222 n6). This, it will be remembered, was precisely the period when Tolstoy was first steeping himself in Chinese philosophy, and the timing of the two developments seems definitely more than fortuitous. Such, at least, is the opinion of the editors of the Jubilee Edition, who comment on this passage: "The project for the *Circle of Reading,* carried out only in 1906 with the appearance of a two-volume anthology published by 'Posrednik,' first became evident in 1884 with the reading of Confucius and Lao Tzu" (*ibid.*).

Let us turn once more to the ten items that relate specifically to China. Several (nos. 4-9) need no further comment at this point.[18] The second, *How the Chinese Live,* is, of course, none other than a shortened redaction for "Pos-

[17] Simmons, *op. cit.,* p. 653.

[18] Passages from some will be quoted in chs. 5 and 6 when we come to evaluate Tolstoy's understanding of China and possible Chinese influence on his own thinking. The *Letter to a Chinese* (item 5) will be discussed in detail in ch. 4.

rednik" of Simon's *La cité chinoise*, which, when read in
Russian translation by Tolstoy in 1887, had so aroused his
enthusiasm.[19] As for the final item, D. P. Konishi's translation of Lao Tzu, it presumably does not greatly differ
from Konishi's translation of the same work which had
originally been published in 1894-95.[20] In 1893-96 the
same Japanese scholar had also published Russian translations of two Confucian works: the *Doctrine of the Mean*
and *Great Learning*. The former quite certainly, and the
latter with fair probability, was known to Tolstoy.[21]

Some interest attaches to Konishi himself (1862-1939).
Arriving in Russia from Japan in 1886, he became a convert of the Greek Orthodox Church, adopted the Russian
name of Daniil Pavlovich (his Japanese personal name was
Masutaro), and entered the theological seminary at Kiev.
While in Moscow in the '90's, he was introduced to Tolstoy
by N. I. Grot, professor of philosophy at the University of
Moscow. Later he returned to Japan, where he was instru-
mental in introducing the works of Tolstoy, with whom he
exchanged several letters from 1896 (September 30) onward. In his later years he seems to have been a professor
at the University of Kyoto.[22]

[19] It was prepared for "Posrednik" by A. A. Gatsuk, a student at
Moscow University. In letters to Chertkov of March 29(?) and April
6, 1888 (JE 86.144-145, 148), Tolstoy complains that though Gatsuk's
plan for redaction was good, the style was far from satisfactory.

[20] See Tolstoy's list of Chinese readings in Appendix B, item 26.

[21] See Appendix B, items 13 and 37.

[22] Biryukov, pp. 143-145, where correspondence between Konishi and
Tolstoy is quoted; Rose Strunsky, transl., *The Journal of Leo Tolstoi*
(*First Volume—1895-1899*), A. A. Knopf (New York, 1917), p. 326
n129; obituary in *Japan Advertiser*, Tokyo, December 28, 1939, p. 2.
The latter states that "in 1895 Mr. Konissi completed the translation
of Lao-tse's *Tao-te-ching* into Russian with the assistance of Count
Tolstoy," but this seems improbable since Konishi had already pub-

Finally, some words about Tolstoy's two unfinished but interesting fragments: *Chinese Wisdom* (item 1) and *Epistle to the Chinese* (item 3). The former comprises three sections, entitled *The Books of Confucius, The Great Learning,* and *The Book of the Way and Truth, Written by the Chinese Sage Lao Tzu.*[23] All three manuscripts are written in identical ink on uniform paper; it is the opinion of the Jubilee Edition editors (*ibid.*, p. 883) that they were composed in 1884 during the initial period of Tolstoy's Chinese enthusiasm. The second and third sections, being merely Russian abbreviated redactions of Legge's and Julien's translations of the *Great Learning* and Lao Tzu respectively, need not detain us further here. *The Books of Confucius,* however, is an original disquisition on Confucian civilization of such intrinsic interest that it deserves quotation in full:

"The Chinese are the oldest people in the world. The Chinese are the most populous people in the world. There are 450 million of them, almost twice as many as Russians, Germans, French, Italians and English put together. The Chinese are the most peaceful people in the world. They seek nothing from others, nor do they wish to engage in war. The Chinese are tillers of the soil. Their ruler himself begins the plowing. And because of that [i.e., because of

---

lished his translation in a periodical of 1894, before republishing it in book form in 1895. See Appendix B, item 26. The confusion may originate from the fact that still a third version of the translation, the one we are here concerned with, was later edited by Tolstoy and published in 1913 after his death. For citation of the *Japan Advertiser* obituary I am indebted to Mr. Richard A. Gard, who refers to it on p. 15 and note 25 of his unpublished M.A. thesis, *The Political Philosophy of Lao Tzu as Expressed in the Tao Te Ching* (University of Hawaii, June 1940).

[23] JE 25.532-533, 533-534 and 534-535 respectively.

their agrarian mode of life], the Chinese are the most peaceful people in the world.

"They say: If a man claims that he is skilled in warfare, know that this man is a great criminal.

"The Chinese live in their own way, not ours. They know how we live but they do not adopt our way of life, for they consider their life to be better. Neither French, Russian, German, Turk nor any other people in the world can, in eating so little and producing so much, compete in work with the Chinese. There is no single people in the world who can till the soil and gain a livelihood from it as well as do the Chinese. Whereas on one *desyatina* [2¾ English acres] a single Russian or two Germans can support themselves, on that same *desyatina* ten Chinese can do so.

"The Chinese have now begun to migrate to America, and the American workers do not know what to do.

"The Chinese work cheaper, better and more honestly than do the latter, but they demand less and so have brought down the wages for all work. Some Americans say: We should accept them. Others say: We should expel them. Like it or not, the work will be taken by him who works better. And he who is better is he who does no harm to anyone, takes less for himself, and gives more to others. The Chinese do no harm, fight with no one, and give more and take less. Therefore they are better. And if they are better, we must find out what is their faith.

"Here is their faith: They say (this is what their teacher Chu-khi says): All men have originated from the Heavenly Father, and therefore there is not a single man whose heart is not endowed with love, virtue, truth, propriety and wisdom. But although natural goodness exists in all people from birth, only a very few can nurture this goodness and

[37]

develop it completely. That is why it so happens that not all people know, or can know, the goodness which lies in them, and develop it. Those, however, who have great sensibility, reason and wisdom, can develop in themselves their spiritual goodness, and it is they who differ from the mass of other people. It is to such men that the Heavenly Father gave a decree to be the leaders and teachers of the people. He decreed that from generation to generation they were to rule and teach the people, so that these might all return to their original purity.

"In this way Fukhi, Chanpunch, Goanti, Iao and Chun received their superior rank from the Heavenly Father, and in this way their assistants carried out their orders. From this their teachings spread everywhere.

"And thus it finally came to be that in the palaces of the rulers, as well as in the smallest hamlets, there was no place where the people did not study. As soon as a boy reached his ninth year—were he the son of an emperor or prince, or of a simple peasant—he entered a primary school where he was taught how to plant, water, cultivate, and keep things tidy. He was taught how to answer politely those who addressed him, how to come forth and greet people, and how to receive guests and see them off. He was taught how to ride horseback, shoot the bow, and how to read, write and count."

What are Tolstoy's sources for this interesting account? The answer is far from certain. Meadows' *The Chinese and Their Rebellions*, for example, which is the only general work on China positively known to have been read by Tolstoy as early as 1884, gives the population of China as 360 million.[24] Where, then, did Tolstoy get his figure of

[24] See above, ch. 2, note 7.

[38]

450 million in the first paragraph? Though popular today, this figure is considerably higher than the estimates found in almost all nineteenth-century books on China.[25] Indeed, of all the books known to have been read by Tolstoy in the early 1880's, there seems to be only one that gives a closely approximate figure, and it, curiously enough, does not specifically deal with China at all, but is Henry George's *Progress and Poverty*. Tolstoy is known to have read this book for the first time in the year 1884,[26] and on one of its pages the statement appears that China has a population of 446,500,000.[27]

The statement in the same paragraph of Tolstoy's essay that "their ruler himself begins the plowing" is a reference to the ceremony (still maintained in Tolstoy's time) in which the emperor, on a certain day each spring, performed the ritual plowing of a sacred field as a signal to his peasant subjects to begin their husbandry. The anti-war saying quoted in the following paragraph is possibly derived from

[25] The figure most usually given is 361 million or thereabouts. Simon's *La cité chinoise* (English ed., p. 3) suggests a population of 400 million for China proper and 537 million for greater China, which is too high. Furthermore, Tolstoy did not read Simon until 1887.

[26] Simmons, *op. cit.*, p. 394.

[27] *Progress and Poverty*, Doubleday & McClure Co. (New York, 1900), p. 113. It is instructive to see how unverified statements of this sort gain wide currency. George's estimate derives from that given in the *Annual Report of the Smithsonian Institution* for 1873, p. 286, which in turn goes back (through an intermediate French source) to that given on p. v of E. Behm and H. Wagner, *Die Bevölkerung der Erde, I*, monograph no. 33 in supplementary vol. 7 of A. Pettermann, *Mitteilungen aus Justus Perthes' geographischer Anstalt*, Gotha, 1872. The only source which Behm and Wagner give for their seemingly precise figure is a general statement by the naturalist, Armand David (who traveled in China, 1864-70), to the effect that China's population must lie somewhere between 400 and 500 million. Cf. Armand David, "Voyage de l'Abbé David en Chine," *Bulletin de la Société de Géographie de Paris*, 6th series, vol. 2 (December 1871), p. 468.

a passage in Mencius in which the latter says: "Those who are skilful to fight should suffer the highest punishment" (*Mencius*, IVa, 14, Legge's translation).

The remarks about Chinese migration to the United States in the fourth and fifth paragraphs reflect Tolstoy's characteristic sympathy for all oppressed groups. At the same time they, together with those expressed in the preceding paragraph, are typical of Tolstoy's economic views. One can imagine the ire with which they would be greeted by any American labor leader today! The events to which they refer are the anti-Chinese movements which agitated the West coast, especially California, during the '60's and '70's, and eventually led to the Exclusion Acts of 1882 and 1891.[28] It is reasonable to suppose that Tolstoy's information on this subject came from his reading of newspapers and similar day-to-day publications. If, however, more specific sources are to be looked for, those that most readily come to mind are certain minor writings of Henry George; but the weight of evidence lies against this hypothesis.[29]

[28] Tolstoy voices concern over the same subject almost ten years after 1884 in *The Kingdom of God Is Within You* (1893): "Ireland and India are subjected to English rule; war is waged against China and the Africans; the Americans expel the Chinese, and the Russians oppress the Jews. . . ." (W 20.197).

[29] Mr. Sergei Polevoy, of the Harvard-Yenching Institute, has suggested Henry George to me as a possible source, and it is true that George did much to crystallize California sentiment against Chinese immigration, both through his article on the subject in the *New York Tribune* of May 1, 1869, and through subsequent California speeches and writings. See Henry George, Jr., *The Life of Henry George*, in *Complete Works of Henry George*, Doubleday, Page & Co. (New York, 1911), vol. 9, pp. 193 and 202. But there is no evidence that Tolstoy ever read these particular writings of George; as for *Progress and Poverty* and *Social Problems*, George's two major works which he did read in 1884, the former contains only three unimportant references to the Chinese in California (pp. 303, 304, 496), and the latter none at all. Professor Ernest J. Simmons, of Columbia University, writes (per-

The sixth paragraph is an interesting, and on the whole quite accurate, summary of certain aspects of Confucian philosophy. Chu-khi, to whom its ideas are attributed, is the famous Neo-Confucianist, Chu Hsi (1130-1200), whose interpretation of Confucianism, embodied especially in his commentaries on the classics, has been generally accepted as orthodox from his day until the last few decades. Despite his enormous prestige in China, he was but comparatively little known in the West as late as 1884. This makes one wonder if Tolstoy may have derived this passage from the longer account of Confucianism appearing in Meadows' book (pp. 342-348), which is there stated to be based upon Chu Hsi's commentaries on the classics. Yet the two accounts, though somewhat similar, do not wholly agree. In particular, Meadows refers to Chu Hsi not as Chu-hi (Tolstoy's Chu-khi) but as Choo tsze (Chu Tzu, i.e., the Master Chu); furthermore, he mentions only two of the names given by Tolstoy in the following paragraph. This indicates that Tolstoy, even if he followed Meadows in part, must at the same time have drawn on some other unreported source.

As a matter of fact, what Tolstoy here attributes to Chu Hsi actually goes back, in large measure, to early Confucianism, and especially to Mencius. Mencius, more than anyone else, was responsible for the doctrine that all men are by nature good, but that only a few are able fully to preserve and develop this innate goodness in later life; and

---

sonal communication of December 22, 1947): "My own guess is that he [Tolstoy] obtained the information from American newspapers or American visitors. Tolstoy received all manner of American newspapers, and, so far as one can tell, he made a practice of reading them."

that to those few, known as sages (*sheng*) and worthies (*hsien*), Heaven confers a solemn trust, known as its "decree" or "mandate" (*ming*, a word also sometimes translated as "fate" or "destiny"), which gives to them the divine right, as long as they show themselves to be morally worthy, to be the rulers and educators of the people. It is interesting that Tolstoy, perhaps under the influence of Christian terminology, has here converted the Chinese "Heaven" (*T'ien*) into a "Heavenly Father." The "love, virtue, truth, propriety and wisdom" with which he says men's hearts are endowed, are, in a slightly changed sequence, the five major virtues of Confucianism: benevolence or human-heartedness (*jen*, Tolstoy's love), righteousness (*i*, Tolstoy's virtue), propriety (*li*), wisdom (*chih*) and good faith (*hsin*, Tolstoy's truth).

In the next-to-last paragraph, Tolstoy enumerates, with some curious spellings, a list of five semi-divine and quite legendary sages, traditionally said to have ruled China in the third millennium B.C. In their correct English romanization they would be Fu Hsi ("Subduer of Animals"), Shen Nung ("the Divine Husbandman"), Huang Ti ("the Yellow Emperor"), Yao and Shun. Tolstoy's transcription of them, as well as of the name of Chu Hsi, suggests fairly strongly that he (or at least the writer, possibly a Russian, whom he used as his immediate source) was basing himself upon a work originally written in French.[30]

[30] This becomes apparent from the following table, in which Tolstoy's transcriptions of these names (divided, for the sake of consistency, into their component syllables) are compared with the modern standard English, French and Russian transcriptions of the same names (the Russian transcriptions being in turn converted from the Russian into the Latin alphabet according to the system used by Ernest Simmons in his *Leo Tolstoy*):

The final paragraph is a curious parody of the picture of ancient Chinese education, itself highly idealized, that we find portrayed in such Confucian works of the last few centuries B.C. as the *Li Chi* (Book of Rites) and *Chou Li* (Rites of Chou). Tolstoy's description agrees with the Confucian accounts in including such subjects as reading, writing, archery and etiquette in the educational curriculum, but its mention of such earthy activities as planting, watering and cultivating is quite un-Confucian, and betrays an unmistakable Western touch. It suggests that Tolstoy was here not drawing upon actual translations of any Chinese source, but upon some secondary European account written by someone who had none too good a knowledge of the original texts.[31]

English	French	Tolstoy	Russian
Chu Hsi	Tchou Hi	Chu Khi	Chzhu Si
Fu Hsi	Fou Hi	Fu Khi	Fu Si
Shen Nung	Chen Noung	Chan Punch	Shen Nung
Huang Ti	Houang Ti	Goan Ti	Khuan Di
Yao	Iao	Iao	Yao
Shun	Chouen	Chun	Shun

It will be noticed that Tolstoy's spellings diverge widely from the standard modern Russian transcriptions, and that they resemble the French transcriptions more closely than they do the English. Particularly important is the second syllable in the names of Chu Hsi and Fu Hsi, for which Tolstoy writes *khi* (analogous to the French *hi*), whereas the standard Russian transcription is *si* (analogous to the *hsi*). Tolstoy's spelling of the fourth name as Goan Ti represents the usual change of initial foreign "h" into Russian "g." As for the extraordinary rendering of the third name, Chan Punch, this can almost certainly be attributed to an error on the part of the Jubilee Edition editors in deciphering Tolstoy's unusually difficult handwriting. The mistake probably arises from the fact that in rapid handwriting, the Russian equivalents of "N" and "P" and "g" and "ch" can easily be confused with one another. That the editors should have committed this error is understandable, but their failure to check with a sinologist, who could easily have set them right, is less excusable.

[31] The Confucian attitude toward "vocational" subjects of this kind

The bald and unpolished style of Tolstoy's *Chinese Wisdom* shows that it was only a rough draft, probably intended for popular consumption. The fact that it remained unpublished suggests that he was dissatisfied with it, perhaps in part because he later realized that its picture of China was not wholly realistic.[32]

Yet another unfinished fragment, the third item in Tolstoy's writings and sponsored publications on China, is his *Epistle to the Chinese*. Begun in 1900, a year which in other ways, as we have seen, was marked by special Chinese interest on Tolstoy's part, this *Epistle* even now remains unpublished save for a tiny excerpt in the Jubilee Edition. Inspiration for its writing came from sad events connected with the Boxer Rebellion of this year. This "rebellion"— actually a violent anti-foreign reaction by the Chinese to a long sequence of Western acts of exploitation in China— resulted in a siege of the foreign legations in Peking which lasted from June 20 until the arrival on August 14 of an

---

is well summed up by Confucius in the *Analects* (XIII, 4): "On Fan Ch'ih [a disciple] requesting to be taught agriculture, the Master [Confucius] replied: 'I am not as good for that as an old husbandman.' When he asked to be taught gardening, he was answered: 'I am not as good for that as an old gardener.' Fan Ch'ih having withdrawn, the Master said: 'What a petty man is Fan Ch'ih! If a superior love good manners, his people will not dare be disrespectful. If he love righteousness, his people will not dare be unsubmissive. . . . If he be like this, the people will come from every quarter carrying their children strapped on their backs. What does he want with learning agriculture?'"

[32] See below, p. 61. Yet one wonders whether it may not have provided the basis for another of Tolstoy's essays which bears the same title and was published by "Posrednik" in 1907 (see p. 32 above, item 5). Unfortunately the latter has not been available for comparison. Hence we must accept the word of JE editors, who state quite definitely that the 1884 *Chinese Wisdom* has been published for the first time in JE vol. 25.

allied force that had fought its way from the coast, some ninety miles distant. The liberation was followed by an orgy of killing, raping and looting on the part of the allied troops, including the Russian detachment under the command of General Linevich. Equally horrible was the wholesale drowning of several thousand Chinese (estimates range from three to seven thousand) which took place at about the same time at Blagoveschensk on the Siberian-Manchurian frontier. This occurred when the Russians, angered and alarmed by Chinese bombardments from across the Amur (July 14-15, 1900), drove thousands of civilian Chinese living on the Russian side of the river to their death in the stream.

These events powerfully moved Tolstoy, and at the end of September, 1900, he first thought about writing an *Epistle to the Chinese* by way of protest. During October and part of November he composed several tentative drafts, none of which, for some unknown reason, was ever completed.[33] The following is a small fragment of one of these drafts—the only one yet published in the Jubilee Edition: "Armed people, calling themselves Christians, are now committing the greatest crimes among you. Do not believe them. These people are not Christians but a gang of the most terrible, shameless criminals, who have never ceased to plunder, torture, corrupt and destroy, bodily as well as spiritually, all working people—nine tenths of the population of Europe and America. And now they wish to lay hands on you, rob you, subject you, and, above all, corrupt you, because without the corruption of those peoples whom they torture, this small gang of robbers would

[33] Gusev, pp. 605-607; JE 54.52-53, 433-434 n140; 72.429 n8, 488 n11.

not have been able to rule over millions . . ." (JE 54.433-434 n140).

In a published article of slightly earlier date, *"Thou Shalt Not Kill"* (August 8, 1900), Tolstoy expresses the same moral indignation. Concerning the Kaiser, who was a leading inciter of the war spirit against China, he writes: "Let him say that in China the army must not take any captives, but must kill all men, and he is not put into a lunatic asylum, but they shout 'Hurrah!' and sail for China to execute his command" (W 23.173-174). Of Czar Nicholas II he writes with equal bitterness: "He finally causes the Chinese slaughter, which is terrible for its injustice, cruelty, and incompatibility with the project of peace, and all people, on all sides, laud him simultaneously for his victories and for the continuation of his father's peaceful policy" (*ibid.*). Similar vehement denunciations of Western imperialism in China appear in several of Tolstoy's published writings of this and neighboring years.[34]

[34] *The Slavery of Our Time* (1900; W 24.25, 52); *What Is Religion?* (1902; W 24.99-100, 110-111); *"Bethink Yourselves!"* (*London Times*, June 27, 1904), in which Tolstoy alludes bitterly to the drowning of the Chinese in the Amur; *Patriotism or Peace* (1896; W 20.477). The latter contrasts the truculence of the Kaiser with the "meekness of Buddha," "wisdom of Confucius," and "humility of Lao Tzu," and quotes an anti-war saying which it attributes to Confucius, but which is paraphrased so loosely that it cannot be identified with certainty.

CHAPTER IV

TOLSTOY'S CONTACTS WITH CHINESE

DESPITE Tolstoy's protracted study of China, it was only in the last five years of his life that he enjoyed personal communication with intellectuals of that country. Concerning the first of these, a certain Chang Ch'ing-t'ung, we know extremely little—little more, indeed, than that, while residing in St. Petersburg (perhaps as a member of the Chinese legation?) he, together with A. N. Voznesenski, translated into Russian a monograph on modern Chinese history that had been written in 1901 by the famous Chinese scholar, Liang Ch'i-ch'ao (1873-1929). This monograph, entitled *Li Hung-chang, or a Political History of China during the Last 40 Years*, was published in St. Petersburg in 1905.[1] As Chang Ch'ing-t'ung is apparently unmentioned in the volumes of the Jubilee Edition hitherto published, we are forced to rely on what is said of him in Biryukov's *Tolstoi und der Orient*,[2] on various pages of which Chang's name appears with the most astonishing variations.[3] From this we learn

[1] See Appendix B, item 7. Li Hung-chang (1823-1901) was one of the most important Chinese statesmen of his day.

[2] Pp. 125 ff. and 177-178 n17.

[3] These variants, given without a word of explanation, are typical of the carelessness which mars Biryukov's book. They are as follows: (1) Tsien Huan-t'ung (p. 125), (2) Tsien Huang-t'ung (pp. 177-178 n17), (3) Tsien-Huang-T'ung (p. 266, index), (4) Tschantschintun (p. 261), (5) Chan-Sien-T'ung (p. 264, index). The fourth variant is most nearly correct. It comes close to Chzanchintun, which is the way Chang's name (in Russian transliteration) appears on the title page of his book; this, according to the standard Wade-Giles transliteration of Chinese words into English, would be Chang Ch'ing-t'ung. Biryukov's Tsien would probably be Ch'ien in the Wade-Giles system. The stand-

that Tolstoy's contact with Chang started when the latter
sent him, from St. Petersburg, a copy of his translation,
together with a letter dated December 1, 1905. In the letter,
after expressing the hope that Tolstoy would read "our
book," Chang comments on certain Chinese philosophical
terms and religious attitudes, among the latter the skepti-
cism felt by most educated Chinese concerning the heaven
and hell spoken of in Christianity.

In a prompt reply of December 4,[4] Tolstoy expresses
delight at Chang's letter, the first, he writes, that he has
ever received from a Chinese. "For a long time now I have
worked fairly intimately with Chinese religion and philosophy, even if, as a European, far from sufficiently thor-
oughly. Quite aside from Confucius, Mencius, Lao Tzu,
and the commentators on them, I have been especially
captivated by the teaching of Mo Ti, against whom Mencius turned himself." Tolstoy then goes on to express sympathy with the Chinese people for their unhappy position in
the Russo-Japanese War (1904-05), and for the repeated
acts of exploitation suffered by them from quasi-Christian
peoples. He remarks, however, that though he has had no
time as yet to read Chang's book, he fears he will be forced
to disagree with its thesis that widescale reform and mod-
ernization are needed in China. Such reform, he points out,
is justifiable only when it springs naturally from a people's
internal development; it should not consist of wholesale
borrowing from the West. The letter then concludes by

---

ard Russian equivalent of Ch'ien would be Tzyan, and, as spelled in
Russian letters, Tzyan and Chzhan (= Wade-Giles Chang) might be
confused fairly easily. It is inexplicable, however, how Biryukov man-
aged to convert Russian Tschin (= Wade-Giles Ch'ing) into Huan,
Huang, or Sien (= Wade-Giles Hsien).

[4] Biryukov, pp. 127-130.

saying: "May God preserve China from the course of Japan.[5] The Chinese, like all of us, should develop their spiritual powers and not strive for technological improvements, which only create harm if the soul be turned the wrong way. I am wholly of your opinion that a spiritual bond exists between the two great peoples, Russian and Chinese, and that they should work hand in hand. But this should not be through political ties or any kind of governmental agreements. Both, and especially their farmers, must work out for themselves a new way of life independently of government. They should not, however, strive for 'freedoms' of all sorts, such as freedom of thought and speech, popular political representation and the like. Rather it should be that true freedom which consists in the possibility of living without any need for government or anything else to decree moral law for them."

The next, and only other, Chinese with whom Tolstoy corresponded was the strict Confucianist and ardent opponent of occidental culture, Ku Hung-ming (1857-1928), whose fluent and prolific writings in European languages have made him widely known in the West. Born in Penang, Malaya, he is said to have studied for nearly twelve years at the University of Edinburgh, followed by a year at Leipzig. Afterwards he went to China, where he held a variety of official and educational posts, including some two decades as secretary of the famous "reformist" viceroy, Chang

---

[5] Tolstoy expresses his strong distrust of Japan several times during these years. Cf. his letter of April 25, 1906, to a Japanese journalist, Tokutomi Kenjiro (Biryukov, p. 158), and letter of September of the same year to Ku Hung-ming (p. 52, below). He manifests the same distrust as early as 1896 in his *Patriotism or Peace* (W 20.477-478), no doubt as a result of Japan's victory in the first Sino-Japanese War of 1894-95.

Chih-tung (1837-1909). In the years immediately following the first World War, his Confucian ideology made a deep impression in Germany, particularly upon the group of political thinkers centered around Leonard Nelson in Göttingen, which was responsible for publishing a number of Ku's essays in German translation. His last years, however, were spent in poverty in Peking, where his unbending conservatism and adherence to an outmoded Confucianism made him an object of derision to his own people.[6]

In 1906 Ku sent to Tolstoy from Shanghai, through the intermediary of the Russian Consul-general, two of his newly published works, both violent denunciations of Western imperialism: *Papers from a Viceroy's Yamen*, and a smaller pamphlet, *Et nunc, reges, intelligite! The Moral Causes of the Russo-Japanese War*.[7] Following their receipt, Tolstoy wrote a lengthy letter in reply, upon which he worked during most of the second half of September, 1906. Under the title of *Letter to a Chinese*, it was published during this and the following year in German, French and Russian.[8] In the letter (too long to be quoted

[6] Biryukov, pp. 178-179; Reichwein, *China and Europe*, p. 10; H. G. W. Woodhead, ed., *China Year Book, 1928* (Tientsin, 1928), p. 1133; Chang Hsin-hai, "Mr. Ku Hung-ming," *The China Critic*, Shanghai, vol. I, no. 1 (May 31, 1928), pp. 12-13; Wen Yuan-ning, "Ku Hung-ming," *T'ien Hsia Monthly*, Shanghai, vol. 4 (1937), pp. 389-390; Francis Borrey, *Un sage chinois, Kou Hong Ming, notes biographiques*, Marcel Rivière (Paris, 1930), pp. 16-18. The latter (p. 89) quotes an interesting remark of Ku that illustrates his conservative and idealized attitude toward his own country: "There are only two really good books on my country: Simon's *La cité chinoise* and M. Hovelaque's *La Chine* [Émile Hovelaque, *La Chine*, Flammarion (Paris, 1920)]."

[7] See Appendix B, items 8-9.

[8] See JE 36.693, 695-696; 55.244, 558 n575; Gusev, p. 685; Biryukov, pp. 178-179. The letter is item 5 on p. 32 above, and should be distinguished from the *Epistle to the Chinese* of 1900 (p. 31, item 3). Its

here in full), Tolstoy begins by saying: "I have received your books and read them with great interest, especially the *Papers from a Viceroy's Yamen*. The life of the Chinese people has always interested me to the highest degree, and I have taken pains to become acquainted with the things in Chinese life which were accessible to me, for the most part Chinese religious wisdom: the books of Confucius, Mencius, Lao Tzu, and the commentaries on them. I have also read on Chinese Buddhism, as well as the books of Europeans on China. . . .

"The Chinese people, who have suffered so much from the immoral, crudely egoistic, and avaricious cruelty of the European peoples, have up to the present replied to all the violence committed against them with a majestic and wise composure, and have preferred patience in the struggle against force. I speak of the Chinese people and not of their government."

Tolstoy goes on to praise China's manifestation of this spirit in 1898, when she ceded Port Arthur to Russia, Kiaochow to Germany, and Weihaiwei to England.[9] Then he says: "The successes of some thieves provoke the envy of others, and the seized prey becomes an object of wrangling and thus brings the thieves themselves to ruin. So it is with dogs, and so also it is with people who have lowered themselves to the level of animals."

For this reason, Tolstoy says, he reads with regret in

Russian version (which is the one followed here) is available in JE 36.290-299; a German version is to be found in Biryukov, pp. 130-142.

[9] He ignores the fact that these "cessions" (more properly leases) were scarcely manifestations of Chinese "patience," but rather of the weakness, corruptness and decadence of the Manchu government then ruling China, which would never have made them unless compelled by overwhelming force to do so.

Ku's book of the rise of a spirit of resistance in China and of a desire there to exact retaliation for European crimes. His regret is not caused by the possibility that China may thus become a danger to Europe. Rather it springs from the fact that China will in the process lose the genuine and practical wisdom that lies in her ordinary people—that folk-wisdom which is rooted in a peaceful agrarian mode of life, such as is natural for all reasonable people to follow, and to which all such people, once it has been lost, must, sooner or later, consciously return.

"I believe," Tolstoy says, "that a great upheaval in the life of humanity is taking place in our time, and that in this upheaval China, at the head of the peoples of the Orient, must play an important rôle. It seems to me that the rôle of the oriental peoples of China, Persia, Turkey, India, Russia, and perhaps also Japan (if it is not completely entangled in the net of the corruption of European civilization) consists in showing to the world the right way to freedom, for which, as you write in your book, the Chinese language has no other word than *Tao*, a way, that is, an activity, which agrees with the eternal fundamental law of human life."

In former times, he continues, the lack of communications made it possible for rulers to exert their direct power only over a small portion of their people. Now, however, because of improved travel and communications facilities, such as the telephone, postal service and telegraph, this power becomes more and more pervasive. The result is an intensification of the evils that have already been generated through the gradual corruption that always accompanies the exercise of power, and this results in turn in a growing awareness among the people of their situation. The rulers of the West, as a consequence, have been forced to accept limitations upon their power in the form of popular representation in government, i.e., the transference of power from the one to the many.

"In our time," Tolstoy comments, "I believe the turn has now come likewise for orientals in general and Chinese in particular to become aware of the utter harm caused by despotic rule and to seek a means of liberation from it, since under present conditions of life it has become intolerable. I know that it is taught in China that the highest ruler, the Emperor, must be the wisest and most virtuous man, and if he is not, his subjects can and should refuse him allegiance. But I believe that this doctrine represents only an excuse for despotism. . . . The Chinese people cannot know whether their emperor is wise or virtuous."[10]

Tolstoy then quotes the dictum of Alexander Herzen, who once remarked that a Genghis Khan would be impossible in the age of the telegraph and electricity, because the added power which these technological developments give a ruler is so conspicuous that the people, becoming conscious of it, would invariably rise in revolt.[11] Nevertheless, Tol-

---

[10] Tolstoy is here referring to the Confucian political theory of the so-called "right of revolution," for which Mencius was in good part responsible. We have already seen (pp. 41-42, above) that, according to Confucian theory, Heaven confers its decree or mandate upon persons who are morally superior, giving to them a divine right to rule the masses. The corollary to this doctrine in China, however, is that this right is retained in a ruling house only as long as its members prove their moral fitness to hold it. Should the sovereign rule badly, Heaven withdraws from him its decree, and thereupon it is legally permissible for the people to revolt and establish a new ruler in his place. This theory, often invoked in the many changes of dynasty that have occurred in China during the past two thousand years, is succinctly embodied in the Chinese term for revolution, *ko ming*, which literally means "changing the decree."

[11] This was said before the days of Hitler and other modern dictators!

stoy argues, though changes in the ancient Chinese despotism are undoubtedly needed, they should not consist of
mere imitation of Western political and social institutions:
"Especially is this true of China because of the peace-lov-
ing character of its people and the poor organization of its
army, which give Europeans the opportunity to plunder
Chinese territory with impunity under the pretext of various clashes and disagreements with the Chinese government. Thus the Chinese people cannot but feel the necessity
of changing their relation to the ruling power. And here I
can see from your book, as well as other sources of information, that some light-minded people in China, called the
reform party, believe that this change should consist of
doing just what the European nations have done, that is, of
replacing a despotic government by a republican one, and
establishing the same kind of army and industry as those of
the West.[12] This decision, which seems at first glance the
simplest and most natural, is not only light-minded but very
stupid, and, from all that I know about China, quite unnat-
ural for the wise Chinese people."

Such a step, Tolstoy continues, would mean the loss of
that way of life which, not only for the Chinese but for all
humanity, constitutes the true and only Way, the *Tao*. Suppose China were to take this step and to expel Europeans.
Such has been precisely the course of Japan, which has
adopted a constitution, strengthened its army and navy,

[12] Though such ideas were held by some of the reformers active in
China at this time, notably Sun Yat-sen, they certainly go far beyond
those of Ku Hung-ming himself (a monarchist who wished to save
China through the spiritual force of Confucianism), as well as of his
master, the mildly "reformist" viceroy, Chang Chih-tung. See Meribeth
E. Cameron, *The Reform Movement in China, 1898-1912* (Stanford
University Press, 1931), esp. p. 42; also Wen Yuan-ning, article cited
in note 6 above.

and developed a modern industry, with consequences that are clear to all: "The position of the [Japanese] people increasingly resembles that of the European nations, and this position is a very difficult one."

Tolstoy argues that the position of the Chinese people, despite the encroachments of imperialism, is still enviable when compared with that of Europeans (by whom he here means in particular the peoples of industrialized Western Europe), among whom bitter struggles are rife between labor on the one hand and government and capital on the other. What is most lamentable, he says, is that these Europeans, because of the very nature of their economic system, are compelled to live parasitically upon the exertions of the food-producing (i.e., agrarian) peoples of China, India and Russia. "And yet the reform party invites you to emulate these parasitical peoples and their activities." Industrialization has caused Europeans to abandon agriculture in favor of the manufacture of unnecessary objects of all kinds. Their position, though outwardly imposing, is doomed unless they give up a mode of life which is based upon deceit, corruption and the exploitation of agrarian peoples.

What, then, Tolstoy asks, should be done? In the case of us Russians, he replies, the answer is clear: We should refuse to obey our present government, but this does not mean that we should merely imitate the West by changing our form of government for theirs. Rather, we should follow our own simple agrarian way of life, and should offer no resistance to any force that is brought against us, since by that very act of resistance we associate ourselves with the violence of the aggressor. And this, too, should be the course of the Chinese. For not only will they thereby free themselves from foreign aggression, but also from the unwise demands of their own government—demands which run counter to China's true moral teaching: "Only hold fast to that freedom which consists in following the wise path of life, the *Tao*. Then all the evils inflicted on you by your officials will vanish of themselves, and the oppressions and plunderings of the Europeans will become impossible. Free yourselves from your officials by refusing to carry out their demands, and above all, by not obediently participating in the plundering and enslavement of one another. Free yourselves from the robberies of the Europeans, by following the *Tao* and not recognizing yourselves as being attached to any state or having any responsibility for the acts of your government. All European annexations and thefts are made possible only when a government is maintained whose subjects you recognize yourselves to be. Were no Chinese government to exist, the foreign countries would be deprived of any pretext to commit their crimes under the guise of international relations."

The root of the evil, Tolstoy goes on to say, lies in the attitude which people hold toward their human ruling authorities: "As soon as people recognize human power as superior to that of God and of His law (*Tao*), they then become slaves; all the more so when that power becomes increasingly complex (as in the case of a constitution which they establish and obey). Freedom can exist only for that people for whom the law of God (*Tao*) is the only supreme law, to which all other laws are subordinate. If you, by refusing to obey your government, will give no help to the foreign powers in their aggressions against you, and if you refuse to serve them, whether it be in a private, civil, or military capacity, then there will be none of those disasters from which you now suffer."

Today, Tolstoy continues, we are passing through a great transition from childhood to adulthood, a transition that consists in freeing ourselves from the unbearable rule of men and establishing our lives on a basis other than that of human power. The peoples of the Orient are well fitted for this transition because they still remain agricultural, retain faith in a superior law of Heaven or God, and have not yet taken over the militarism and industrialism of the Occident. What is essential, then, is that the peoples of the Orient should seek for freedom, not by creating such pseudo-limitations upon governmental power as are found in popular representation, but by following that divine law or *Tao* which excludes obedience to a merely temporal power.

Tolstoy concludes his letter with the following exhortation: "May the Chinese people but continue to live their peaceful, industrious, agricultural life as they have before, behaving in accordance with the fundamentals of their religions: Confucianism, Taoism and Buddhism, all three of which basically agree on liberation from all human power (Confucianism), not doing to others what you do not wish to be done to yourself (Taoism), and self-abnegation, humility and love to all people and creatures (Buddhism). Then all those disasters from which they suffer will automatically disappear, and no power will be enough to conquer them."[13]

[13] Here Tolstoy seems inadvertently to have confused Confucianism with Taoism. It is the latter and not the former that seeks for liberation from all human power, since it regards governmental institutions as corrupters and distorters of man's original goodness. Confucianism, on the contrary, recognizes the necessity for government, though it insists

This long letter is a wonderful expression of Tolstoy's matured political philosophy; some of its utterances are remarkably prophetic of the problems that now confront us even more urgently than they did in Tolstoy's day, however much readers may disagree with Tolstoy's solution. Two years after its writing, Tolstoy's contact with Ku Hung-ming was briefly renewed when the latter sent him his translations of the *Doctrine of the Mean* and the *Great Learning*.[14] Commenting on them in his diary of October 26, 1908, Tolstoy remarked that they "provoke thought."[15]

---

it should be one founded upon a balanced harmony, in which the social obligations and privileges held by each individual are clearly delimited according to his particular station in life. Furthermore, it was Confucius and not the Taoists who proclaimed the negative version of the golden rule: "Do not do to others what you do not wish yourself" (*Analects*, xv, 23).

[14] See Appendix B, items 16-17.   [15] JE 56.152, 513-514 n397.

CHAPTER V

THE MEANING OF CHINA TO TOLSTOY

HERETOFORE we have been concerned with the factual story of how and when Tolstoy studied China and Chinese thought. Though some of its details are made obscure by the fact that not all sources have yet been published, its main outlines are clear. Our next task—in many ways more difficult, because less concerned with concrete fact—is an evaluation of the ideological significance that these studies had for Tolstoy. In what spirit of inquiry did he approach his subject? How accurate was his understanding of China? What were the elements in it that especially attracted him?

In the first place, it is obvious that Tolstoy's approach was far from "scholarly" or "scientific." Numerous factual inconsistencies and errors can be detected in what he writes at various times. In 1862, for example, he sets the population of China at 200 million;[1] in 1884 at 450 million;[2] and in 1887 (or possibly also in 1884) at 360 million.[3] In 1890, after having used James Legge's *Chinese Classics* for some six years as his primary source for Confucianism, he confesses to Chertkov that he is unable to remember the name of its author.[4] The same letter betrays uncertainty as to the dates of Mo Tzu, by suggesting that not only Mencius, but possibly Confucius as well (who antedated Mo Tzu), refuted his arguments. In 1900 Tolstoy is so impressed

[1] *Progress and the Definition of Education* (W 4.162).
[2] See p. 36 above.   [3] See p. 16 and note 7.
[4] See p. 28. Yet who has not had a similar temporary lapse of memory at one time or another!

with the *Great Learning* that he takes the trouble to sum-
marize it in his diary; in so doing, however, he wrongly
entitles it the *Doctrine of the Mean*.[5] And on several occasions he attributes both the *Doctrine of the Mean* and the
Great Learning to Confucius, though Legge, in his prolegomena to these works, states clearly that they could not
have come from Confucius himself.[6]

There is nothing surprising in these errors, for to Tolstoy they are inconsequential details, having no intrinsic
importance. What he is interested in are the ideas in the
books he reads, and not such questions as their date and
authorship. Often, therefore, he seems to use the name of
Confucius as a convenient label under which to lump all
the early Confucian writings. This, perhaps, is why he
mentions Confucius so frequently and Mencius compara-

[5] Diary, December 8, 1900 (JE 54.70). The JE editors, in their comment on this passage (JE 54.448 n181), fail to notice this error—one all
the more striking in view of the fact that in another diary entry of
November 12, 1900 (JE 54.55-62), Tolstoy clearly indicates his awareness of the difference between the two works.

[6] Legge, *Chinese Classics*, I, 26, 36. The *Doctrine of the Mean* is
commonly attributed to Tzu-ssu, the grandson of Confucius, and the
Great Learning either to Tzu-ssu or to Tseng Tzu, a disciple of
Confucius. Though the latter attributions are open to some question, it
is certain that neither work was written by Confucius. See Fung
Yu-lan, *A History of Chinese Philosophy*, translated by D. Bodde,
vol. I (Peiping, 1937), pp. 362, 369-370. Tolstoy, in his diary of March
23, 1884 (see p. 21 above), attributes the *Doctrine of the Mean* to Confucius; in the section on the same work in his *Chinese Wisdom*, he
likewise says that "this book was written by the Chinese sage Confucius"
(JE 25.533). In his *On Life* (1888; W 16.244) he puts what is apparently a paraphrase of the opening sentence of the *Doctrine of the Mean*
into the mouth of Confucius; again, in his diary of November 19, 1900,
he quotes another sentence from it, which he calls "the teaching of
Confucius" (JE 54.63). No doubt Tolstoy was helped in his false
attributions by the fact that Konishi, in his translations of the *Doctrine
of the Mean* and the *Great Learning*, indicates, by the very titles of his
translations, his belief that they are both the work of Confucius. See
Appendix B, items 13 and 37.

tively rarely, even though the latter's idealistic tendencies must undoubtedly have appealed to him.[7]

When it comes to the broader concepts that underlie Chinese civilization, however, Tolstoy's understanding is quite remarkable for one who is not an avowed China "specialist." We have already seen (pp. 37-38, 41, 53) that he understood correctly the orthodox Confucian theory of society and government: all men are born good; only a few of them, however, are able to preserve this goodness; these few are given a "decree" or "mandate" by Heaven to rule and care for the masses; but if they rule badly, Heaven withdraws this decree and it then becomes legitimate for the people to revolt and establish new rulers in their place.

In his first enthusiasm for China, Tolstoy seems to have accepted this theory without question.[8] In later years, however, no doubt as the result of a growing disbelief in the goodness of *any* government, no matter how "benevolent," he strongly denies its validity. "This doctrine," he writes to Ku Hung-ming in 1906, "represents only an excuse for despotism. . . . The Chinese people cannot know whether their emperor is wise or virtuous" (p. 53 above). There is more than a grain of truth in this criticism, and with it we see how Tolstoy moves away from the overly idealistic view of Chinese civilization inspired by such books as those of Meadows and especially Simon.[9] From 1893 onward, in

[7] Among Tolstoy's few references to Mencius are those on pp. 22, 28, 48, and 51 above, and these say little of his actual doctrines. Yet Tolstoy's interest in Mencius is shown by his direct praise of him on p. 22, as well as by his indirect allusions to his doctrines on pp. 37-38 (see also pp. 41-42) and p. 53 (see note 10).

[8] *Chinese Wisdom* (1884). See above, pp. 37-38.

[9] Another equally idealistic work, hitherto unmentioned, is Georgiyevski's *Principles of the Life of China* (St. Petersburg, 1888), which leans heavily on Simon and similar writers. It does not seem to have come into Tolstoy's hands before 1900, however. See Appendix B, item 5.

fact, he repeatedly rejects, either explicitly or implicitly, the Chinese theory that their rulers are infallible.[10]

Tolstoy also knows enough about the religions of China to realize that there is a vast difference between them as philosophical systems and as institutionalized cults; between Taoism as a philosophy, for example, and Taoism as a popular religion. In China, as elsewhere, he points out, a religion usually pays for its material success by spiritual degeneration. Such degeneration may be observed "in exalted Buddhism, which, with its monasteries and representations of Buddha, and its endless solemn rites, has changed into the mysterious Lamaism; in Taoism, with its sorcery and incantations."[11]

What was it that made Tolstoy feel so akin to the Chinese people? In part, no doubt, it was the warm and repeatedly expressed sympathy which he felt toward all peoples who were victims of Western imperialism. But more specifically it seems to have been the qualities of pacifism, frugality, industriousness, and simplicity of living for which he lauds them, quite justly, in his *Chinese Wisdom*.[12] Underlying all these qualities, however, was a basic social and economic consideration: the fact that China was a great *agrarian* country, made up in large part of hardworking peasants. The simple and close-to-earth life of these peasants was, in Tolstoy's eyes, far superior to the corruptions, artificialities and class struggles which he saw in the industrialized countries of Western Europe, with their

[10] *The Kingdom of God Is Within You* (1893; W 20.173-174, 246-247); *Epilogue to "Drozhzhin's Life and Death"* (1895; W 19.501); *Patriotism and Government* (1900; W 23.155).

[11] *What Is Religion?* (1902; W 24.88). Cf. also *Religion and Morality* (1894; W 19.521-522); *The Christian Teaching* (1897; W 22.420).

[12] See above, pp. 36-37.

great factories and crowded urban communities. In this agrarian mode of life, he recognized a factor of basic importance which not only linked China with Russia, but also brought these two nations into spiritual kinship with the other great agrarian countries of Asia, especially India. This point of view appears clearly in Tolstoy's reaction to Simon's *La cité chinoise*, in his own *Chinese Wisdom*, and in his correspondence with Chang Ch'ing-t'ung and Ku Hung-ming. The letter to the latter, in particular, is noteworthy for the unequivocal way in which it groups Russia with the countries of the Orient, in opposition to those of Europe (i.e., Western Europe).[13]

In China itself, Tolstoy found the highest spiritual expression of this "genuine" way of life in the Confucian writings and the book of Lao Tzu. It is time now to examine how he approached these two systems of thought. The editors of the Jubilee Edition sum up the reasons for his interest in Confucius as follows: "Tolstoy's interest in Confucius can apparently be explained chiefly by the fact that the teaching of the Chinese philosopher was devoid of all that is vague, transcendental and miraculous. He was not interested in abstract problems or questions of religious metaphysics, but concentrated himself exclusively on the problem of practical morality and the fundamentals of human society. The high humaneness, and the doctrine of self-negation and love for others, which mark the teaching of Confucius, closely approached the ideas on these subjects held by Tolstoy himself" (JE 25.883).

This statement is confirmed if we examine the way in which Tolstoy uses the sayings of Confucius in his own

[13] See above, pp. 19, 36-37, 48-49, 52. This fact has already been pointed out by Biryukov, p. 252.

writings. Among those which he singles out for quotation is Confucius' famous answer to the disciple who asked about the meaning of death;[14] Confucius' definition of knowledge as something to be grasped through practical intuition, without recourse to epistemology or logic;[15] his statement emphasizing the importance of personal moral example;[16] and his enunciation in negative form of the golden rule.[17] It is obvious that the simplicity and directness of the Confucian approach to morality, with its constant stress upon individual self-improvement as the key to the betterment of society as a whole, made a great appeal to Tolstoy. Thus on several occasions he expatiates approvingly upon the famous "eight steps" for moral development which form the basis of the *Great Learning*.[18]

[14] "Not yet understanding life, how can you understand death?" (*Analects*, XI, II). See Tolstoy, *Thoughts and Aphorisms, I. Religion* (1892; W 19.80).

[15] "When you know a thing, to know that you know it, and when you do not know it, to recognize that you do not know it: this is knowledge" (*Analects*, II, 17). To which Tolstoy adds: "But false knowledge consists in thinking that we know what we do not know, and do not know what we know. It is impossible to give a more exact definition of that false knowledge which reigns among us." See his *On Life* (1888; W 16.283).

[16] On being asked by a ruler how it would do to execute the lawless for the good of the law-abiding, Confucius replied: "What need, sir, is there of capital punishment in your administration? If your desire is for the good, the people will be good. The moral character of the ruler is the wind; the moral character of those beneath him is the grass. When the grass has the wind upon it, it assuredly bends" (*Analects*, XII, 19). Quoted in *Thoughts and Aphorisms, I. Religion* (W 19.81).

[17] "Do not do to others what you do not wish yourself" (*Analects*, XV, 23; also V, II). For Tolstoy's use of this saying, see above, p. 57 and note 13; also *The Only Means* (1901; W 23.244-245).

[18] Cf. Tolstoy's *Chinese Wisdom*, sect. 2, *The Great Learning* (JE 25.533-534), and his diary, entries of November 12 and December 8, 1900 (JE 54.55-57, 70). The "eight steps" are (1) the investigation of things, (2) extension of knowledge, (3) making of the thoughts sincere,

There is another, more mystical, side to Confucianism, however, which not only insists upon self-cultivation as an act in itself, but emphasizes that the validity of all human moral values rests, in the final analysis, upon other values that transcend the purely human sphere; the ultimate goal of man's moral cultivation, therefore, is to apprehend these higher values and thus gain union with the divine forces which give him being. This concept, which is fundamental in Mencius' insistence upon the innate goodness of human nature (based upon the premise that the nature is conferred upon man by Heaven), appears also in the *Great Learning* and, more especially, in the *Doctrine of the Mean*. There is no doubt that it appealed deeply to Tolstoy's religious convictions.[19] Thus he writes in 1884: "In the book of Confucius it says: 'The law of the great science [i.e., great learning] consists in developing and establishing the principle of the light of reason, which we received from heaven.' This proposition is repeated several times and serves as the foundation of the teaching of Confucius."[20]

Again he writes in 1892: "In all the moral teachings there is established that ladder which, as Chinese wisdom

---

(4) rectification of the mind, and (5) (moral) cultivation of the person; these, successively carried out, lead to (6) the proper regulation of the family, (7) good government of the state, and finally (8) attainment of universal peace. For Tolstoy's use of other sayings from the *Great Learning*, similarly emphasizing the importance of personal moral cultivation, see ch. 2, note 28, and *Thoughts and Aphorisms, VIII. Dissatisfaction* (1886; W 19.155).

[19] See his praise of Mencius and comment on his teaching on pp. 22-23 above.

[20] *My Religion* (W 16.107). This "quotation" is really Tolstoy's own free interpretation of the opening sentence in the *Great Learning*. It occurs with only slight verbal changes in his exposition of the *Great Learning* (also written in 1884 and cited in note 18 above).

says, extends from heaven to earth, and which cannot be ascended except by beginning with the lowest rung."[21]

Yet there are other aspects of Confucianism of which Tolstoy could hardly have approved, and which are closely related to its social and political background. When studying Confucianism, it is important to remember that it first emerged in China's age of "feudalism"—a crumbling feudalism, to be sure, and not wholly the same as that of Europe, but one, nonetheless, in which the old class distinctions still remained strong. Confucius and his followers, though clearly recognizing that something was wrong in the operation of the society of their time, did not question the fundamental validity of this society itself. The fault, as they saw it, was functional rather than structural, and could, they sincerely believed, be repaired through an act of moral regeneration.

It is possible, therefore, to interpret the rise of Confucianism as an attempt on the part of some of the more farsighted intellectuals associated with China's ruling class to revitalize the traditional institutions and beliefs—then in a state of transition—by injecting into them new moral interpretations. This motivation appears to us today a good

[21] *The First Step* (W 19.368). This seems to be another free interpretation, apparently of the passage in the *Doctrine of the Mean*, ch. 22, descriptive of the sage: "It is only he in the world who has the most perfect sincerity who can develop his nature to the utmost. Able to develop his own nature to the utmost, he can do the same to the natures of other men. Able to develop to the utmost the natures of other men, he can do the same to the natures of things. Able to develop these to the utmost, he can assist the transforming and nourishing operations of Heaven and Earth. Capable of assisting in their transforming and nourishing operations, he can form a trinity with Heaven and Earth." Another paraphrase, probably of the opening sentence of the *Doctrine of the Mean*, occurs in Tolstoy's *On Life* (1888; W 16.244): "'Life is the dissemination of that light which came down from heaven for the good of men,' Confucius said, six hundred years before Christ."

deal more clearly than it did to most Westerners of the nineteenth century. Even by the early Confucianists themselves, in fact, it was probably hardly consciously sensed in the bald terms in which it is outlined here. Nevertheless, its influence may be seen in the essentially aristocratic point of view which Confucianism retained in later times despite extensive modifications when it became the orthodoxy of an age of empire. Throughout its later history, in fact, it has been primarily the ideology of a privileged ruling class, and only secondarily that of the people as a whole. The great distinction between it and similar ideologies in other civilizations is that membership in the ruling class in China was not determined solely by the accident of birth, but depended in good part on certain intellectual and moral attainments. Much of Confucianism has been a formulation of the standards that were demanded from the class of moral "gentlemen" to justify their positions as rulers over the uneducated masses.

The result, politically speaking, was a benevolent but paternalistic form of government, the success of which depended upon the degree to which all members of society willingly accepted their proper social status and behaved accordingly. As Confucius himself said: "The people may be made to follow a path of action, but not to understand the reason why" (*Analects*, VIII, 9). We have already seen how Tolstoy strongly criticized this doctrine of the infallibility of the elite ruling class.

A good deal of Confucianism, too, has been concerned with the detailed rules of etiquette that should govern the relationships of the class of moral gentlemen. It is one of the hallmarks of this class that it should appreciate the "higher" cultural and aesthetic values. Confucianism, as a consequence, has usually avoided asceticism and welcomed the "good things" of life: on the higher plane, accomplishments like music, art, and literary skill; on the lower, such niceties as good food and clothing—always provided, however, that they are not pursued to the exclusion of moral values. It is obvious that some of these concepts, despite the accompanying stress on moderation, conflict with Tolstoy's own disdain for ceremonial show of any kind, and his rather puritanical tendencies toward self-renunciation and asceticism, evinced, for example, in his vegetarianism and preaching of sexual chastity. When confronted by such elements as these which do not readily accord with his own ideology, Tolstoy usually solves the problem they create by simply ignoring them. This technique, as we shall see, generally characterizes his approach to all of the philosophies and religions which interest him.

It appears, for example, in Tolstoy's attitude toward Taoism, in which he eagerly seizes upon certain ideas that particularly appeal to him, while seemingly ignoring others. The editors of the Jubilee Edition comment on the attraction which Lao Tzu had for him as follows: "In this book [the *Tao Te Ching* of Lao Tzu], Tolstoy was especially attracted by the preaching of bodily abstinence and of spiritual self-perfection which should form the basis of human life" (JE 25.883). This statement is well confirmed by Tolstoy's own comments on and quotations from Lao Tzu. "Meekness" and "humility" are repeatedly stressed as the basis of Lao Tzu's philosophy, and by way of support Tolstoy quotes (or rather paraphrases) such sayings as "The sage unto the end never makes a show of greatness and thus achieves his greatness" (chs. 34 and 63), "The wise are not learned, the learned are not wise" (ch. 81), and "What is strong and great holds the lower place; what is tender and weak holds the higher place" (ch. 76).[22] It is easy to see how such statements would be welcomed by Tolstoy, with his dislike for show and self-aggrandizement, distrust of formal learning, and deep belief in the Christian doctrine of humbleness summed up in Christ's words: "Blessed are the meek: for they shall inherit the earth."

In Taoism, however, as in Confucianism, Tolstoy was not satisfied merely to seek for self-perfection on the human plane. He looked further for a clue to that higher spiritual force which he believed with his whole being underlies all human activity and gives it its meaning and justification. In the case of Taoism, he did not need to seek far, for the essence of Lao Tzu's philosophy is that underlying the universe, as we see it, there is an absolute first cause or principle, called the *Tao* or Way, from which all being is evolved, and to the eternal laws of which man must conform if he is to gain enlightenment and true happiness. Tolstoy's emphasis on this spiritual aspect of Taoism is well brought out in his essay, "On the Essence of Lao Tzu's Teaching," written for the booklet on Lao Tzu published by "Posrednik" in 1910.[23] In this he says:

"The foundation of his teaching is the same as that of all the great and true religious teachings. It means: Man first of all recognizes himself as a corporeal being, distinct from all others and filled only with egoistic desires. But

[22] *On Life* (1888; W 16.244) ; *Thoughts and Aphorisms, III. Form and Existence* (1892; W 19.115-116) ; letter to Chertkov of September 21, 1893 (JE 87.223-224) ; *Patriotism or Peace* (1896; W 20.478) ; diary of August 8, 1907 and notebook of the same month (JE 56.52, 251) ; statement of December 27, 1907 (JE 56.473 n223).

[23] See above, p. 32, item 6.

besides the fact that the individual man considers himself
to be a Peter, a John, a Mary or a Catherine, he also recognizes each as an incorporeal spirit which lives in all beings
and gives life and growth to all forms of existence. Thus
man may exist either as a physical personality, distinct
from all others, or as an incorporeal spirit which moves in
him and desires the growth of all existing things. Man can
live either for his body or for his soul. If he lives for his
body, his life is a continual suffering, inasmuch as the body
endures pain, becomes ill and dies. But if he lives for his
soul, his life is blessed, inasmuch as for the soul there is no
suffering, no illness and no death. . . .

"According to the teaching of Lao Tzu, the only way for
man to unite with God is through *Tao*. *Tao* is achieved by
abstinence from all that is personal and corporeal. The same
teaching is to be found in the First Epistle of Saint John,
and just as, by the word *Tao* in Lao Tzu's teaching, is to
be understood not only the means of uniting oneself with
Heaven, but also Heaven itself, so, according to Saint
John, by the word love is to be understood not only love,
but also God himself. (God is love.) The essence of both
teachings consists in the fact that man can conceive of
himself as either separate or indivisible, body or spirit,
temporal or eternal, animal or divine. In order to gain
consciousness of oneself as spiritual and divine, there is,
according to Lao Tzu, only one means, which he defines
with the word *Tao*, a word which also includes in itself the
idea of the highest virtue."[24]

This passage illustrates the way in which Tolstoy unconsciously reads into the philosophies he studies the ideas

[24] JE 36.697; Biryukov, pp. 244-245. Only the second paragraph is
found in the JE citation.

which he himself wishes to find there. In some ways it is a penetrating analysis of certain aspects of Lao Tzu's thinking. Yet at the same time it reveals a subtle but unmistakable difference—one that rests, in the final analysis, on the fact that Lao Tzu's view of the universe is naturalistic, while that of Tolstoy is theistic. This fact emerges most clearly from the way in which Tolstoy interprets the word *Tao*.

The *Tao*, as conceived by Lao Tzu, is the first principle or cause from which everything in the universe takes its being; as such it is all-sufficient, all-perfect, and ineffable. "We do not know its name," he says, "so we term it *Tao*" (ch. 25). Yet it is not on that account to be interpreted as a conscious creator of the universe. There is in it no trace of personality, conscious volition, or "goodness" as opposed to "evil," at least in the way in which these last two terms are ordinarily used. (For Lao Tzu, they and all similar value judgments are man-made concepts which have no absolute validity from the viewpoint of the *Tao*.) The *Tao* includes in itself both body and spirit, being and non-being; it transcends and at the same time is immanent in the universe as we see it. In short, *Tao* is the name for the totality of all those natural and immutable laws whose spontaneous operation causes the universe, both seen and unseen, to be as it is; *Tao*, in fact, is itself the spontaneous.

To the scientist there is nothing either morally "good" or "bad" in the fact that all creatures are born and all must some day die; this is simply one of the laws of nature or, as the Taoists would say, of the *Tao*. On this point the ancient Taoists would certainly agree with the modern scientist. Of these laws of *Tao*, perhaps the most fundamental is that of reversal or return: everything that goes to one extreme must some day pass to the other; what flourishes must eventually decay. This is the real reason why "the world's weakest overwhelms the world's hardest" (ch. 43), and "what is high is brought down, and what is low is raised up" (ch. 77). It is not because there is a conscious Power that wills it so.[25]

Hence when Tolstoy equates *Tao* with Heaven, and through this term with God, this in itself could not be objected to, if by "God" he really meant a naturalistic principle similar to what Lao Tzu and the other Taoists intended when they used the term *T'ien* or "Heaven." When, however, he introduces the love of Saint John into his equation and when, furthermore, he creates a dichotomy between spirit and body and advocates "abstinence from all that is personal and corporeal," it is obvious that his view of Taoism has been colored by his own Christian spectacles.[26] Tolstoy's insistence on the theistic import of Lao Tzu's philosophy already appears in his first attempt at translation in 1884, in which he renders *Tao* as God.[27] This insistence is the more remarkable in view of his dependence then, and for some years to come, on the French translation of Julien, who strongly denies that *Tao* has any theistic

[25] For a good account of Lao Tzu's philosophy, see Fung Yu-lan, *A History of Chinese Philosophy*, vol. 1, ch. 8; also Introduction of Arthur Waley, *The Way and Its Power*, Allen & Unwin (London, 1934). The latter is the best English translation of the *Tao Te Ching*, and has been consulted (though not invariably followed) in the quotations here given.

[26] Though Lao Tzu several times speaks of the importance of eliminating the desires, he does not mean by this a complete denial of basic physical needs, but only of those morally corrosive desires that come with sophisticated living. This is shown by his prescription for the people living in his ideal society: "Let them obtain their food sweet, their clothing beautiful, their homes comfortable, and their rustic tasks pleasurable" (ch. 80).

[27] See his *Chinese Wisdom*, sect. 3, *The Book of the Way and Truth* (JE 25.534-535).

significance whatever.[28] It explains also his intense interest
in the German translation of Victor von Strauss, which in
1893 he used as the basis for a Russian version of his own,
despite V. V. Stasov's justified criticism of Strauss as a
"theosophist" who renders *Tao* as God.[29]

Another important aspect of Lao Tzu's philosophy—his
views of government and society—seems to be ignored by
Tolstoy in his direct quotations and observations. This
topic, however, will be discussed in detail in the following
chapter.

By now we are better able to understand the spirit in
which Tolstoy approached the Chinese sages and, in the
same manner, the major world religions and philosophies
generally. As a seeker for religious truth, he was ill-
equipped either by temperament or training to study his
subject with the fastidious attention to detail of the pro-
fessional scholar. Such an approach, indeed, was for him
typical of "that false knowledge which reigns among us."[30]
His own method was simple: to seek from each system of
thought those concepts which he felt represented universal
truths, while brushing aside the infinite variations in their
expression as insignificant detail. If in the process he
sometimes unconsciously allowed his own ideals to intrude
and subtly transmute the ore which he thus extracted, he
also no doubt succeeded better than most men in realizing
that certain ideas are basically important, precisely because

[28] Julien, *op. cit.*, p. xiv: "In *Lao-tzu* and the earliest members of his
school before the Christian era, the use and definition of the word *Tao*
exclude all idea of an *intelligent cause.*"

[29] See above, pp. 24-25, and *Stasov*, pp. 107, 109. In his *Letter to a
Chinese* (1906), Tolstoy likewise speaks of *Tao* as "the law of God."
See above, p. 56.

[30] See note 15 above.

they have been expressed and re-expressed so often in the most varied times and places, and therefore offer the greatest hope of bringing harmony to a divided mankind.

His own view on this subject is perhaps best summed up in a letter which he wrote in the last year of his life:[31] "From a knowledge of other religions . . . people will see that in all great religions, in addition to the one which they themselves profess, there exist two kinds of religious affirmations: those which have infinite differences and variations, depending on the time, place and character of the people among whom they have appeared; and those others which are the same for all religions. They will see that not only must one believe in these latter universal affirmations, but that it is impossible not to do so, inasmuch as in addition to being the same for all religions, they have been written down in the heart of every man as unquestionable and joyous truths. This is why I think that here, especially in our own time, the communicating to people of the main foundations of all the great religions of the world is a most necessary task."

[31] Letter of February 24, 1910, to V. A. Posse (JE 85.374).

CHAPTER VI

THE QUESTION OF CHINESE INFLUENCE

THE time has now come to ask a final question: Did Tolstoy's study of Chinese thought leave any perceptible influence on his own ideas? A precise answer is obviously difficult in view of what has just been said. Nevertheless, there are at least three lines of thought which would seem to merit further exploration. They are Tolstoy's theory of music, theory of the state and of nonresistance, and theory of immortality.

1. *Theory of Music.* Tolstoy, as is well known, was rigorously moral in his judgment of music. Music, he maintained, is, of all the arts, the most potent, for under its spell men can become completely bereft of their own senses. If improperly used, therefore, it can be a dangerous weapon for evil. Some music, however, is purifying and morally good. Such is the case with folk-music, for example, since it is the spontaneous and unsophisticated expression of the lives of the people as a whole. But there are other "higher" and more sophisticated kinds of music which fall into quite a different category, being nothing more than the esoteric productions of a small group of intellectuals who write only for their own master-class and have no roots in the common people. Music of this kind reflects nothing but the artificial lives and decadent ideology of this restricted group and so has no universal validity. At best it is unintelligible to most of those who hear it; at worst it corrupts and destroys moral standards. The real test for any musical composition, therefore, is not its aesthetic or sensuous ap-

peal to a select master-group, but the degree to which it is comprehensible to all and at the same time is morally elevating. This reasoning, as is well known, leads Tolstoy into some remarkably harsh condemnations which include "all of Bach and all of Beethoven with his last period," as well as "Wagner, Liszt, Berlioz, Brahms, Richard Strauss, and so forth, and all the enormous mass of entirely useless imitators of these imitators."[1]

Tolstoy's theory of music, with which is associated his moralistic theory of art in general, has often been attributed to the influence of Plato.[2] The similarity between the two men is indeed considerable. Nevertheless, if we turn to what the Confucianists of ancient China said on the same subject, we find there a similarity that is, if anything, even more striking. For music, to these Confucianists, is one of the major supports of any well-ordered state. Its function in society is that of providing a safety valve for human emotion which, unless thus permitted release, can cause definite psychological harm to the individual. The direction taken by this emotion when it is released, however, is of prime consequence; unless carefully guided in orderly fashion along the correct moral path, it may lead to uncontrollable license and disorder. The true criterion for music, therefore, is its inner moral content rather than its superficial attractiveness. The early sage-kings, realizing this fact, were careful to create only that music which would lead their people along the proper moral path. In later times, however, many persons have unfortunately rejected

[1] *What Is Art?* (1897; W 22.253).

[2] Israel Knox, "Notes on the Moralistic Theory of Art: Plato and Tolstoy," *International Journal of Ethics*, vol. 41 (1931), pp. 507-510; David Kvitko, *A Philosophic Study of Tolstoy* (New York, 1927), pp. 105-108.

this classical form of art in favor of the more exciting "licentious airs" of such states as Cheng and Wei.

Such is the sophisticated theory that was elaborated by the Confucianists of the third and second centuries B.C.[3] Several centuries before, however, we find Confucius praising the moral purity of the ancient music and condemning the licentiousness of the new.[4] The following passage from the *Li Chi* or *Book of Rites* is a good brief expression of the theory in its later development: "The early kings, when they instituted . . . music, did not do so to gain full satisfaction for the desires of the mouth, stomach, ears and eyes. But they intended to teach the people to regulate their likes and dislikes, and to turn them back to the normal course of humanity. . . . When man is acted upon by external things without end, and no regulation is set to his likes and dislikes, he becomes changed through the encounter with any external object. To be so changed . . . is to have the natural principle within him extinguished, and to give the utmost indulgence to his human desires. With this there comes the rebellious and deceitful heart, with its licentious and wild disorder. . . . Therefore the early kings instituted . . . music to regulate human conduct."[5]

Let us turn now to Tolstoy's famous fictionalized description of what he considered to be the immoral effect of certain music:[6]

" 'They were playing the Kreutzer Sonata by Beethoven,' he [Pozdnyshev] continued. 'Do you know the first presto? . . . Ugh! Ugh! That sonata is a terrible thing. . . . Music,

[3] See Fung Yu-lan, *History of Chinese Philosophy*, vol. 1, pp. 341-344.
[4] *Analects*, III, 25; xv, 10; xvII, 18, etc.
[5] See translation of Legge (here modified) in *Sacred Books of the East*, vol. 28 (Oxford, 1885), pp. 96-97.
[6] *Kreutzer Sonata* (1889; W 18.390-391).

in general, is a terrible thing. . . . They say that music acts upon the soul by elevating it—nonsense, a lie! It acts, acts terribly, . . . but not at all by elevating. It neither elevates nor humbles the soul—it irritates it. How shall I tell it to you? Music makes me forget myself and my real condition; it transfers me to another, not my own condition: it seems to me that under the influence of music I feel that which I really do not feel, that I understand that which I do not understand, that I can do that which I cannot do. . . . This music immediately, directly transfers me to the mental condition in which he was who wrote that music. I am merged in his soul, and am with him carried from one condition to another; but I do not know why this happens to me. He who wrote it . . . knew why he was in such a mood; this mood led him to do certain acts, and so this mood had some meaning for him, whereas for me it has none. Therefore music only irritates. . . . It is for this reason that music is so terrible and often acts so dreadfully. *In China music is a state matter. That is the way it ought to be.*[7] How can anyone who wishes be allowed to hypnotize another, or many persons, and then do with them as he pleases? And especially how can they allow any kind of an immoral man to be the hypnotizer?' "

Though we have no concrete evidence that Tolstoy ever read the *Book of Rites*, the reference here to China is conclusive proof that he was at any rate acquainted with the Confucian theory of music from other sources. By contrast, it is a curious fact that "Tolstoy never mentions

---

[7] Italics mine. The real meaning of this passage is that music, in China, is controlled by the state; it is rendered accordingly in Alexander Nazaroff, *Tolstoy, the Inconstant Genius*, Stokes (New York, 1929), p. 259: "In China music is controlled by the State, and it is exactly so that it ought to be."

Plato as his godfather, as he does Socrates," though, so it is argued, "there is . . . a kinship between them."[8] Such a kinship is undeniable in the attitude of Plato and Tolstoy toward music, and the probable influence of the one upon the other would not be contested here. Yet surely it is significant that when Tolstoy utters one of his most famous indictments of the immoral effect of certain kinds of music, he does not support it by the familiar example of Plato's *Republic*, but turns instead to distant China. Is it reasonable to suppose that he would have done so if the Confucian moral approach had not impressed him at least as profoundly as that of the Greek philosopher?[9]

2. *Theory of the State and of Non-Resistance.* Tolstoy, as we have already seen, strongly condemns the artificialities and corruptions that emerge as by-products of organized society, especially when men are torn from their "natural" way of life on the soil and herded into great cities to become slaves of the machine. It is therefore natural that government itself should be included in his general condemnation. This view has been summed up by one scholar as follows: "It is in the very nature of governments to infringe upon human rights, especially rights of freedom, using the sanction of a few mighty, and some 'learned' advisers. . . . Nor does the particular form of government

[8] Kvitko, *op. cit.*, p. 105.

[9] This inference has, to my knowledge, been hinted at (though without elaboration) only by Tolstoy's English translator, Leo Wiener, who writes in his "Analysis" of Tolstoy's life and works (W 24.303) : "The idea of the immoral effect of music is as old as Plato and the Chinese sages." Reichwein, to be sure, also refers to China in connection with Tolstoy's attitude to music. In so doing, however, he does not go to Confucianism at all, but quotes an isolated saying from Lao Tzu (ch. 35) which is really irrelevant. See Reichwein, *China and Europe*, p. 8.

matter; a monarchy differs from a republic but little. From its very nature no form of rule can be good, for it is organized violence; and that is worse than individual assault. . . . 'Majority Rule' to Tolstoy, as to any anarchist, is no justification of government."[10]

The similarity of these views to those of Lao Tzu is striking. The Chinese thinker, confronted by the profound social and political upheavals of the age in which he lived (fourth or third century B.C.), found the source of these troubles in the fact that man, by his ceaseless creating of the complex artifacts and institutions of "civilization," has upset the natural order of the universe, the *Tao*. And the further man thus isolates himself from the original natural harmony, the more do his activities serve to aggravate the chaos they are designed to prevent. As Lao Tzu says: "The more restrictions and prohibitions there are in the world, the poorer the people will be. The more sharp weapons the people have, the more troubled will be the country. The more cunning craftsmen there are, the more pernicious contrivances will appear. The more laws are promulgated, the more thieves and bandits there will be" (ch. 57).

The only solution is to reduce human institutions and government to a minimum, so that man may return to that condition of pristine innocence in which he once lived long ago. Though Lao Tzu does not go so far as to advocate the abolition of government entirely—a step taken by some of his followers—he does envisage a form of society in which people would live a simple life in small rural communities, and in which boats, carriages and writing, though not unknown, would be voluntarily put aside. "The neigh-

[10] Kvitko, *op. cit.*, p. 39. See also Tolstoy's condemnation of government on pp. 52-57 above.

boring state might be so near at hand that one could hear the cocks crowing in it and the dogs barking. But the people would grow old and die without ever having been there" (ch. 80).

It is curious that Tolstoy, though politically an anarchist, seems never to allude by name to this anarchistic strain in Lao Tzu's philosophy. Solid evidence exists, none the less, to show that Lao Tzu was known to the anarchist circles of Western Europe of Tolstoy's day.[11] Is it reasonable to suppose that Lao Tzu's political philosophy could have been ignored by Tolstoy himself, for whom this Chinese thinker was an avowed "favorite"? On the contrary, the link between the two is found in Tolstoy's *Letter to a Chinese*, in which, though without specifically mentioning Lao Tzu, he appeals directly to the Chinese *Tao* as support for his own anarchistic ideas.[12]

[11] Cf. the following articles: "Le Taoisme et la philosophie des premiers anarchistes," *La Paix*, Paris, August 16, 1892; same title in *Le Genêvois*, Geneva, August 17, 1892; "Un vieil ancêtre des anarchistes," *Chronique Parisienne*, Paris, May 15, 1892; "Un vieil ancêtre des anarchistes, Lao-tse," *Journal de Beaugé*, June 10, 1892; Albert Delacourt, "Lao-tse, père de l'anarchisme en Chine," *Revue Blanche*, Paris, September 1, 1897, p. 395. All these titles are listed in Gard, *The Political Philosophy of Lao Tzu* (cited in note 22 of ch. 3 above), p. 13 n 18.

[12] See above, pp. 54, 56-57. By other scholars Tolstoy's political anarchism has been traced to the influence of Rousseau. See Kvitko, *op. cit.*, pp. 84-87; Milan I. Markovitch, *Jean-Jacques Rousseau et Tolstoï*, Honoré Champion (Paris, 1928), esp. pt. 3. Here again I would not try to deny this influence but, as in the case of music, would point to China as at least an equally important co-stimulus. As a matter of fact, it is not wholly impossible that Rousseau himself may in some respects have been influenced by Chinese thought—not, however, that of Taoism, which in his time was little known in Europe, but of certain Confucian writers, especially Mencius, who may themselves have been somewhat tinged by Taoist ideology. This, at least, has been suggested by E. R. Hughes, *The Great Learning and the Mean-in-Action*, E. P. Dutton (New York, 1943), pp. 22-31, 176.

An important element in Lao Tzu's political philosophy is what he calls *wu wei*, literally "non-activity." It does not really mean the complete absence or avoidance of activity, however, but only of such activity as does not accord with the universal *Tao*; in other words, of all activity that is forced, artificial and self-assertive, rather than natural, spontaneous and unpremeditated. As such, *wu wei* may often be rendered as "non-assertion."

By Lao Tzu the term is used primarily to describe the conduct of the ideal sage-ruler who, wishing to follow the *Tao*, reduces his machinery of government to a minimum and refrains from any attempt at forcibly imposing his will upon his people. "I act not (*wu wei*) and the people of themselves are transformed," says Lao Tzu (ch. 57). "The sage relies on actionless activity" (ch. 2). "If he practise non-activity, there is nothing that is not well governed" (ch. 3). Therefore, Lao Tzu urges, "Be subtracted and yet again subtracted, till you have reached non-activity. Then through this non-activity there will be nothing unaccomplished" (ch. 48).

This concept (under the name of *le non-agir* given it by Julien in his translation) strongly impressed Tolstoy. In taking it over, however, it is characteristic that instead of stressing its predominantly political significance, he "Christianized" it into a means whereby every individual may morally perfect himself and so carry out the acts of God. Thus he defines it as follows in a letter of March 12, 1889, to Chertkov: "I like very much the saying: '*Dans le doute abstiens toi.*' I consider this to be a wise Christian rule. It is the same as the highest virtue in Lao Tzu, '*le non-agir.*' As I understand this, all our sins come from what we do, that is, from doing for ourselves what we ought not to have done. It is only what we cannot help but do, however, that is God's doing—the work done by God through us and by means of us. Were man to abstain from all personal acts, other acts would still remain from which he would be unable to abstain, and these would be the acts of God. If, however, man busies himself with his own activities, then because of these and of the turmoil they produce, he fails to see or recognize the acts of God. Therefore one must act only when one cannot help but do so. . . . Yes, only when one goes deep within oneself and abstains from one's personal wishes, does the work of God, which we are called upon to do, become clear" (JE 86.218).

In another letter to Chertkov of April 27, 1893 (JE 87.190), Tolstoy reverted to the same subject, and in the same year he even wrote an article which he called "*Le non-agir*" or "*The Non-Acting*." In this, the occasion for which was a dispute in France between Zola and Dumas regarding the attitude that should be taken to science, Tolstoy attacked all forced activities done without any thought as to their true purpose, and supported Dumas in his appeal to youth to put its faith in brotherly love rather than science. The use which Tolstoy makes in this article of Lao Tzu's *wu wei* doctrine appears in the following passage: "There is a little known philosopher, Lao Tzu (the best translation of his book, *Of the Road of Virtue* [*sic*], is that by Stanislas Julien). The essence of Lao Tzu's teaching is this, that the highest good of individual men, and especially of the aggregate of men, of nations, can be acquired through the knowledge of 'Tao,'—a word which is translated by 'path, virtue, truth'; but the knowledge of 'Tao' can be acquired only through non-acting, '*le non-*

agir,' as Julien translates it. All the misfortunes of men, according to Lao Tzu's teaching, are due, not so much to their not having done what is necessary as to their doing what they ought not to do. And so men would be freed from all personal and especially all social misfortunes—it is the latter that the Chinese sage has more especially in mind—if they practised non-acting (*s'ils pratiquaient le non-agir*)" (W 23.49).

This passage, in which Tolstoy correctly indicates the importance Lao Tzu gives to *wu wei* in the social sphere, leads naturally to his own famous doctrine of political non-resistance. Admittedly, this theory stems in the first instance from his Christian views, yet it seems undeniable that it also received much support from his readings in other religions and philosophies.[13] Indeed, he implies as much in one of his letters to Gandhi.[14] Among these influences, Taoism surely emerges as one of the most conspicuous, especially when, in addition to the *wu wei* doctrine itself, we remember such sayings of Lao Tzu as "Requite enmity with kindness" (ch. 63), and "The good I treat as good, but the ungood I also treat as good. . . . The truthful

---

[13] Markovitch, *op. cit.*, p. 256, largely disregards the question of Christian influence and attributes Tolstoy's doctrine primarily to Rousseau: "Is it not justified to conclude . . . that Tolstoi has drawn at least the first notions of his doctrine of non-violence from the reading of Rousseau?"

[14] Letter of September 7, 1910 (Biryukov, p. 73): "This law [of non-resistance] has been promulgated by all the sages of humanity: Hindus, Chinese, Hebrews, Greeks and Romans. It has been, I believe, expressed most clearly by Christ, who has said in precise words that this Law contains all law and the Prophets." It is well known that Tolstoy's theory of non-resistance (which, however, as we have seen in his *Letter to a Chinese*, did not exclude civil disobedience on the part of the people to their government) had a great influence upon Gandhi's civil-disobedience campaigns and passive-resistance doctrine.

I treat as truthful, but the untruthful I also treat as truthful" (ch. 49).[15]

3. *Theory of Immortality.* Though much of Tolstoy's thought is rooted in Christianity, he broke decisively with the conventional Christian view in his rejection of the doctrine of a continued personal existence after death. His own attitude toward the problem of immortality has been summarized as follows: "Tolstoy found that calm and peace were impossible unless one renounced concern for his individuality here and in the beyond. But from this perishable part—individuality—man is delivered with death. The spiritual part, on the other hand, being immaterial is indestructible. Since the living God is the Whole of which man's soul is a part dwelling in a perishable body, with death the part returns to the Whole. Death, then, becomes a good, not an evil, and the fear of death vanishes in the light of reason. . . . Renunciation of earthly life does not, for Tolstoy, mean entering into a new individual life hereafter or retribution of the righteous beyond the grave, as the priests teach. . . . Tolstoy quotes the Synod as charging that 'He does not acknowledge a life and retribution beyond the grave!' and replies, 'If one is to understand, by life beyond the grave, the Second Advent, a hell with eternal torments, devils, and a Paradise of perpetual happiness—it is perfectly true that I do not acknowledge such a life beyond the grave. . . .'

"What, then, is death? It is a transformation into a state in which there is no desire, no separate existence, but instead complete absorption in God. Pain and death then

[15] This has already been suggested very briefly by Reichwein, *op. cit.*, p. 5.

cease, being in reality only illusions of this our present separate existence."[16]

This doctrine is ascribed by the scholar just quoted to Hindu, or more strictly speaking, Buddhist influence: "This outlook on death and immortality has, indeed, very little [that is] Christian about it; it is much closer to Buddhism. Why Tolstoy calls it Christian can be explained only by the supposition that Tolstoy interpreted the Sacred Scriptures in the light of Hindu philosophy." Again: "The last named [Tolstoy's concept of immortality] is scarcely to be distinguished from Nirvana." And further: "Had not Tolstoy been so close to Buddhist ideas, he could not have disposed so easily of the Christian survival dogma."[17]

It is reasonable to suppose that Buddhism exerted a considerable influence on Tolstoy's thinking, for we know that he read extensively on that religion. Yet the strong resemblance of Tolstoy's concept of immortality to non-Buddhist Chinese views on the subject is also striking. The Chinese attitude has been summarized as follows: "It is a really remarkable fact that, for millennia, China has been a stronghold of the so-called worship of ancestors, a cult presumably based upon a belief in the immortality of the soul; that it has been a country in which superstitious beliefs in spirits and ghosts of all kinds are rife among the common people; and yet that, when we study what China's sophisticated thinkers have had to say on the subject, we find either that they have hesitated to admit the possibility of immortality at all, or have conceived of it

[16] Kvitko, *op. cit.*, pp. 21-23.
[17] *Ibid.*, pp. 23, 25, 26.

only in general semi-pantheistic terms, rather than in terms of a personal survival."[18]

Though this statement applies to Confucianists as well as Taoists, the pantheistic conception is particularly true of the latter: "The general attitude of the Taoists toward immortality may be summed up as follows: In the universe there is only one all-embracing stream of existence (called the Way or *Tao*); life and death are merely differing phases of this single existence; after death, therefore, we continue to exist as integral parts of this single stream of existence which never dies, but this in no way may be interpreted as signifying a personal form of immortality."[19]

That Tolstoy became aware of this Chinese concept at the very beginning of his studies on China, and absorbed it, together with that of the Hindus, when formulating his own attitude toward the subject, is proved by what he writes in *My Religion* (1884). In this he remarks that the idea of a personal life after death "is a very low and gross conception," not present in early Christianity. Yet, he continues, we like to prove our self-assumed superiority to other races by the very fact that we accept such a belief, "while others, like the Chinese and the Hindoos, do not keep it" (W 16.125).

Tolstoy could hardly have acquired his understanding of the Chinese approach to the problem merely by reading Lao Tzu or the Confucian "Four Books," for it gained clear-cut expression in China only after these works had been written.[20] Therefore we must conclude that it came

---

[18] Derk Bodde, "The Chinese View of Immortality: Its Expression by Chu Hsi and Its Relationship to Buddhist Thought," *Review of Religion*, vol. 6 (1942), pp. 373-374.

[19] *Ibid.*, p. 375.

[20] Confucius was a skeptic regarding the spirits of the dead, but he

to him from some one of his general readings on China. Meadows' *The Chinese and Their Rebellions* immediately comes to mind, and in it we are indeed told in one place that the Chinese are atheists (p. 361), and in another that the Confucianists say nothing of a life after death (p. 419). Yet it was in January, 1884, that Tolstoy put the finishing touches to *My Religion*, whereas we do not hear of him reading Meadows until later on, July 9-13 of the same year. This is another of the several pieces of evidence tending to prove that the list of Tolstoy's readings on China, as given in Appendix B of this book, is incomplete.

We have now reached the end of our attempt to trace the impact of China upon Tolstoy's thinking, an impact almost certainly broader than the three specific instances here examined, yet impossible to define with the clear-cut precision one would like. Even in these three instances, in fact, we have seen that the ideas of the Chinese sages have been taken into Tolstoy's mind in conjunction with other strains of thought as diverse as Christianity and Buddhism, Plato and Rousseau.

If our results are not fully conclusive, it is because the study of ideas is inherently far more uncertain and open to dangerous conclusions than is the study of material things. Even such a fragile artifact as paper, for example, can be traced with much greater certainty from its invention in China (traditionally A.D. 105) through its passage to the Islamic world (751) and entry into the European

---

did not explicitly deny their existence. In note 14 of ch. 5 we have seen how Tolstoy quoted Confucius' famous remarks about death. The same paragraph in the *Analects* (XI, 11, which Tolstoy then goes on to quote) also records Confucius' answer to the question of a disciple as to how one should perform one's duty to the spirits: "When still unable to do your duty to men, how can you do your duty to the spirits?"

world (twelfth century), than can the transmission of the countless ideas recorded upon it at various times and places.

In the case of Tolstoy, moreover, the situation is greatly complicated by the complexity of the man himself. If he had confined his interest to a single civilization—say that of China—the task would be simple. But Tolstoy would not have been satisfied with such a limitation, for the very validity of his thought rested, in his eyes, upon what he deemed to be its universality. At the same time that he was studying Chinese philosophy, therefore, he was also probing incessantly into the "wise thoughts" of the sages of many other times and peoples, and continually assimilating what he thus found into his own ideology. What has been said of Rousseau in a similar connection applies to Tolstoy equally well: "As with so many great, original minds, the source of what went into him was largely immaterial to him. Anything and everything was grist to his mill, and, when it had been ground in his unconscious mind, it came out as Rousseau and no one else."[21]

Tolstoy, indeed, may be likened to a deep lake fed by many sources. Some are great rivers flowing from distant places, some mere rivulets. Some are swift, some sluggish; some clear, some turbid. Some, indeed, are underground springs, unseen to the human eye. The water in the lake cannot be said to be that of any particular stream or spring; yet it is the water of all of them in their totality. Among these sources that fed Tolstoy's thinking, that of China, exotic and unfamiliar as it was to his contemporaries, was surely, to the Russian sage himself, one of the richest and most rewarding.

[21] Hughes, *op. cit.*, p. 30.

APPENDIX A

A CHINESE POET'S PILGRIMAGE TO
YASNAYA POLYANA

JOURNEY IN THE SOVIET UNION[1] is the title of a recent book (in Chinese) by the noted poet and archaeologist Kuo Mo-jo (born 1892), long an admirer of Soviet Russia and today one of the staunchest supporters of the new People's Government in China. The work records Kuo's travels in Russia in the summer of 1945, when he attended the celebration of the 220th anniversary of the founding of the present Soviet Academy of Sciences. Its interest for us lies in Kuo's detailed description (pp. 176-195) of the two days (August 6-7) spent by him at Tolstoy's estate, Yasnaya Polyana.

In these pages Kuo speaks at length of Tolstoy's interest in China, though without contributing much that is new. Of primary importance is his statement that Dr. Larionov, the curator of Yasnaya Polyana, was at that time writing a study of Tolstoy's contacts with China. We greatly regret having been unable to discover whether this manuscript has since been published. Kuo's own information, largely gleaned from Larionov, contains several errors. These, however, may in part be attributable to his difficulties in understanding Russian and the fact that he is hard of hearing.

[1] *Su-lien Chi-hsing*, Monograph 3 of the Sino-Soviet Cultural Co-operation Society, Chung-Wai (Sino-Foreign) Publishing Co., Peiping, 1946. I am indebted to Mr. Constantine Kiriloff of Peiping for drawing it to my attention (after the present book had been written) and for loaning me his copy.

Concerning Lao Tzu, Kuo writes (pp. 184-185) that in 1909 Tolstoy held daily discussions with the Japanese scholar D. P. Konishi; these resulted in the Konishi-Tolstoy version of Lao Tzu that was published after Tolstoy's death in 1913. This statement disagrees with our own information (see above, p. 35 and note 22), according to which Konishi first met Tolstoy in the 1890's; actively collaborated with him, according to one source, in 1895; and had apparently returned to Japan by 1896. The discrepancy can be reconciled, however, if we assume that Konishi paid a second visit to Russia in 1909. This, if so, would explain why the result of his collaboration appeared as late as 1913.

Kuo further remarks that in Tolstoy's study he saw the Carus translation of Lao Tzu (see Appendix B, item 27), bearing the penciled notes of Tolstoy, and beside it a manuscript by Tolstoy which is presumably the basis for the Tolstoy pamphlet on Lao Tzu published in 1910. The latter, also seen by Kuo, has on its cover a picture depicting the legend according to which Lao Tzu, late in life, departed from China for Central Asia riding on an ox.

Concerning the *Shih Ching* or *Book of Odes* (now one of the Confucian classics), a compilation of popular folksongs and court poetry from the earlier half of the first millennium B.C., about which we have hitherto said nothing, Kuo quotes from Dr. Larionov: "He [Tolstoy] delighted in the *Book of Odes* and recognized that 'in this book one reaches the highest fullness of human life.'"[2]

As to the mysterious Chang Ch'ing-t'ung, with whom Tolstoy corresponded in 1905, Kuo goes on to suggest

---

[2] Kuo, *op. cit.*, p. 185. Tolstoy read this classic in the English translation of Legge. See Appendix B, item 12.

that this name is an error for that of Chang Chih-tung (1837-1909), the famous statesman under whom Tolstoy's other Chinese correspondent, Ku Hung-ming, served for some two decades. This hypothesis is impossible, however, because, as we have already seen (ch. 4, note 3), the name appears as Chang Ch'ing-t'ung on the title page of the latter's book which he sent to Tolstoy together with his letter.

When Kuo Mo-jo left Yasnaya Polyana, he was asked to write some words in the visitor's book and obliged with the following inscription, ingeniously combining homage to Tolstoy with praise of Lenin and Stalin:

"Like a pilgrim, I have come to Yasnaya Polyana to breathe the pure atmosphere left by the great wise man, and have here come to realize more concretely Tolstoy's lofty personality. Although his study, bedroom, living room and books all remain silent, they seem to tell me: 'The Master has just gone out. He is even now walking in the woods.'

"All is so simple, natural, orderly and impressive. These spacious and pure surroundings are not unworthy to be Tolstoy's cradle, or the cradle of such great productions as *War and Peace* and *Anna Karenina*.

"All is preserved naturally. All is preserved for the people. Here in these surroundings it is easier for men to understand the greatness of that vast love of his for the peasants and for all mankind.

"Unceasingly people come here to visit. If Tolstoy has consciousness, I believe it certainly makes him smile. Those lines of sadness, deeply engraved on his face, have probably already disappeared.

"From far and near come the scholars, thinkers and

[93]

creators of all lands. It is not for naught, for it causes them to ponder more deeply: What is the meaning of life? How can our existence be perfected?

"But at the same time I realize more concretely the greatness of Lenin and Stalin, for it is under their leadership that this treasure of mankind has been preserved. All is for the people. They have caused this rich cultural relic to be left as a teaching, not only to their own people, but to all mankind.

"For these overflowing thoughts of love for fellow countrymen and mankind, I from my heart sincerely express my gratitude."[3]

In return, Tolstoy's granddaughter, then at Yasnaya Polyana, presented Kuo with a book describing the place, in which she wrote:

"On the happy occasion of Mr. Kuo Mo-jo's visit to the home of Tolstoy I send love and respect to the people of China.

Tolstaya Esenina"

[3] Kuo, *op. cit.*, pp. 194-195.

APPENDIX B

F OR a discussion of the thirty-nine books, pamphlets and periodicals that follow, see chapter 2. Thirty-two can be definitely proved to have passed through Tolstoy's hands at one time or another; the remaining seven "uncertain items" are so designated either because they cannot be precisely identified, or because, though referred to in correspondence between Tolstoy and others, it is not known for certain whether they actually reached him or not. Items prefixed by an asterisk are those listed in Biryukov, *Tolstoi und der Orient*, pp. 258-263. Whenever available, further documentation has been added from other sources, by means of which it has usually been possible to determine the year in which the item in question first came to Tolstoy's attention. Arrangement within each group below follows this chronological arrangement (indicated by the dates on the left margin), except for those items for which such information is lacking, which have then been arranged according to original dates of publication, with dates on left margin omitted. In compiling this list, much use has been made of the Cordier and Skachkov bibliographies on China (items 12-13 in our Bibliography) to complete the bibliographical data on many items which are cited incompletely or even inaccurately in Biryukov or the original Russian sources.

I. GENERAL AND MISCELLANEOUS (NOS. 1-10)

*1884 1. Meadows, Thomas Taylor, *The Chinese and Their Rebellions, Viewed in Connection with Their Natural*

Philosophy, Ethics, Legislature, and Administration.
Smith, Elder & Co. (London, 1856)
[Gusev, p. 316.]

1887 2. Simon, G. Eugène, *La cité chinoise*, Nouvelle Revue
(Paris, 1885)

[JE 86.145 n5. Tolstoy read this in the Russian translation of
V. Rantsev, *Sredinnoye tsarstvo, osnova kitayskoi tsivilizatsii*
(The Middle Kingdom, the Basis of Chinese Civilization), A.
Panteleyev (St. Petersburg, 1886).]

1900 3. Pauthier, M. G., *Chine moderne, ou description his-
torique, géographique et littéraire de ce vaste empire,
d'après des documents chinois*, 2 vols., Firmin-Didot
Frères (Paris, 1873; 1st ed., 1837-53)

[JE 54.436 n149. All of this is by Pauthier, except vol. 2, pt. 2,
on art, literature and customs, which is by Antoine Bazin.]

1900 4. Vasilyev, V. P., *Religii vostoka: Konfutsianstvo,
Buddism i Daosism* (Religions of the East: Confucianism, Buddhism and Taoism), V. S. Balashev (St. Petersburg, 1873)

[JE 54.436 n149. Originally published in *Zhurnal Ministerstva
Narodnovo Prosveshcheniya* (Journal of the Ministry of Public
Education), April-June, 1873 (vols. 166, pp. 239-310; 167, pp.
29-107, 260-293).]

1900 5. Georgiyevski, Sergei, *Printsipy zhizni Kitaya. Vero-
vaniya, khramy predkov. Brak. Rodovyie nachala. Konfutsi i Konfutsianstvo. Razvitiye Konfutsianstva v ki-
taiskoi literature i provedeniye v zhizn* (Principles of the
Life of China. Beliefs, Ancestral Temples. Marriage.
Tribal Principles. Confucius and Confucianism. Development of Confucianism in Chinese Literature and Its Ap-
plication to Life), I. N. Skorokhodov (St. Petersburg,
1888)

[JE 54.436 n149.]

1900 6. Müller, F. Max, *The Religions of China, I. Confucianism, II. Taoism, III. Buddhism and Christianity*, in

Nineteenth Century, vol. 48 (1900), pp. 373-384, 569-581, 730-742

[JE 54.436 n149. These articles are reprinted in *Last Essays by the Right Hon. Professor F. Max Müller, Second Series, Essays on the Science of Religion*, Longmans, Green & Co. (London & New York, 1901).]

*1905 7. Liang, Ch'i-ch'ao, *Likhunchzhan, ili politicheskaya istoriya Kitaya za posledniya 40 let* (Li Hung-chang, or a Political History of China during the Last 40 Years), translated from the Chinese by A. N. Voznesenski and Chang Ch'ing-t'ung, V. Berezovski (St. Petersburg, 1905)

[See also Biryukov, p. 125. Liang's original work, written in 1901, can be found in his *Yin-ping-shih Ho-chi* (Collected Works), sect. entitled *Chüan-chi* (Collected Monographs), Chung Hua Book Co. (Shanghai, 1936).]

1906 8. Ku, Hung-ming, *Papers from a Viceroy's Yamen; A Chinese Plea for the Cause of Good Government and True Civilization in China*, Shanghai Mercury Press (Shanghai, 1901)

[JE 36.290, 693.]

*1906 9. Ku, Hung-ming, *Et nunc, reges, intelligite! The Moral Causes of the Russo-Japanese War*, Shanghai Mercury Press (Shanghai, 1906)

[JE 36.693.]

1910 10. *The World's Chinese Students' Journal*, bi-monthly, Shanghai, no. 4 (1910)

[JE 58.39, 364 n555; Gusev, p. 771. The JE editors state that Tolstoy made penciled notes on the article, "The Civilization of China," on pp. 219-220 of this journal.]

II. CONFUCIANISM (NOS. 11-18)

—— *11. Faber, Ernest, *A Systematical Digest of the Doctrines of Confucius, According to the Analects, Great Learning and Doctrine of the Mean*, translated from the German by P. G. von Moellendorff, China Mail Office (Hongkong, 1875)

1884 12. Legge, James, *The Chinese Classics; Translated into English with Preliminary Essays and Explanatory Notes*, Trübner & Co. (London, 1867-76) :

> Vol. I. *The Life and Teachings of Confucius*
> Vol. II. *The Life and Works of Mencius*
> *Vol. III. *The She king; or the Book of Poetry*

[JE 54.426-427 n106. This edition is a partial reprint from the original edition of *The Chinese Classics*, 5 vols. (Hongkong, 1861-72), in which *The She king* is the fourth instead of the third vol.]

1896 13. Konishi, D. P., *Konfutsi. Seredina i postoyanstvo* (Confucius. The Doctrine of the Mean), Moscow, 1896
[JE 54.436 n150. It appeared first in *Voprosy Filosofii i Psikhologii* (Problems of Philosophy and Psychology), September, 1895, pp. 381-403.]

—— *14. Karyagin, K. M., *Konfutsi, yevo zhizn i filosofskaya deyatelnost. Biograficheski ocherk* (Confucius, His Life and Philosophical Activity. A Biographical Sketch), Pavlenkov, 2nd ed. (St. Petersburg, 1897; 1st ed., 1891)

—— *15. Whitney, Thomas, *Confucius, The Secret of His Mighty Influence, His Views upon the Great Problem of Human Life and Destiny*, Siebert, Wernich & Quetsch (Chicago, 1900)

[Biryukov states that this contains penciled notes by Tolstoy.]

1908 16. Ku, Hung-ming, *The Universal Order, or Conduct of Life*, Shanghai Mercury Press (Shanghai, 1906)
[JE 56.408, 513-514 n397. This is a translation of the *Doctrine of the Mean*; it is reprinted in Wisdom of the East Series as *The Conduct of Life, or the Universal Order of Confucius*, John Murray (London, 1908).]

1908 17. Ku, Hung-ming, *The Great Learning of Higher Education*
[JE 56.408, 513-514 n397. This, together with the preceding item, was received by Tolstoy from Ku on October 25, 1908, but the JE editors assign it no date or place of publication, nor have I been able to determine them, despite inquiries to many persons and institutions. Mr. Henri Vetch, Peiping publisher and book seller, informs me, however, that he once had a copy and remembers it as a rather small pamphlet which was perhaps published (in a

very small edition) in Tsingtao, China. That it is a translation of
the *Ta Hsüeh* or *Great Learning* is shown by Ku's earlier remarks in the Introduction to his *Conduct of Life* (London, 1908),
pp. 8-9: "The present book [i.e., the *Conduct of Life*], together
with the *Ta Hsüeh*, translated by Dr. Legge as *The Great Learning* or, as it should be properly rendered, 'Higher Education,'
forms what may be called the catechism of the Confucian teaching.
It was my intention to publish these two books together. But I
have not been able to bring my translation of the other book into a
shape to satisfy the standard at which I aim."]

*1909 18. Pauthier, G., *Les livres sacrés de l'Orient, com-
prenant le Chou-king ou le Livre par excellence, les Sse-
chou ou les quatre livres moraux de Confucius et de ses
disciples, les lois de Manou, premier legislateur de l'Inde,
le Koran de Mahomet*, Panthéon Littéraire (Paris, 1852;
1st ed., 1843)

[Gusev, p. 736.]

III. TAOISM (NOS. 19-28)

1884 19. Julien, Stanislas, *Lao Tseu Tao Te-king, Le Livre
de la Voie et de la Vertu composé dans le vi° siècle avant
l'ère chrétienne par le philosophe Lao-Tseu*, Imprimerie
Royale (Paris, 1842)

[JE 25.883.]

1893 20. Chalmers, John, *The Speculations or Metaphysics,
Polity, and Morality, of "the Old Philosopher," Lau-
tsze*, Trübner & Co. (London, 1868)

[*Stasov*, pp. 102-106, 116.]

1893 21. Strauss, Victor von, *Lao-tse's Tao Te king*, Fried-
rich Fleischer (Leipzig, 1870)

[JE 87.224 n2; *Stasov*, pp. 102-107, 109, 112, 151.]

1893 22. Harlez, C. de, *Textes taoistes*, E. Leroux, Annales
du Musée Guimet, vol. 20 (Paris, 1891)

[*Stasov*, pp. 102-106, 109, 151. This translates portions of the
Chuang-tzu, Lieh-tzu, etc., as well as Lao Tzu's *Tao Te Ching*.]

1893 23. Legge, James, *The Texts of Taoism*, vol. 39 of *The*

Sacred Books of the East, edited by F. Max Müller, Clarendon Press (Oxford, 1891)

[*Stasov,* pp. 112, 116, 118, 120, 151. This translates Lao Tzu's *Tao Te Ching* and chaps. 1-17 of the *Chuang-tzu.*]

*1893 24. Rosny, Léon de, *Le Taoïsme*, E. Leroux (Paris, 1892)

[*Stasov,* pp. 102-106.]

1893 25. Pauthier, M. G., *Le Tao-Te-King, ou le Livre révéré de la Raison suprême et de la Vertu, par Lao-tseu*, vol. 1 (only vol. published), F. Didot (Paris, 1838)

[JE 87.236, 237 n5. This states that Tolstoy requested V. G. Chertkov to send him this book, but not that Tolstoy actually received it. Tolstoy was almost surely acquainted with it, however, in view of the many other books on Lao Tzu which he studied in this same year, and the fact that in his letter he familiarly refers to it simply as "Pauthier."]

—— 26. Konishi, D. P., *Laosi. Tao-teking* (Lao Tzu. Tao-te-ching), Moscow, 1895

[JE 36.697; 54.535 n465. Originally published in *Voprosy Filosofii i Psikhologii* (Problems of Philosophy and Psychology), May, 1894, pp. 380-408. Though the JE references do not state categorically that Tolstoy actually read this work, this is proved by the fact that the version of it that was reprinted in 1913 was edited by Tolstoy. See ch. 3 of the present book.]

—— *27. Carus, Paul, *Lao-Tze's Tao Teh King, Chinese-English*, Open Court Publishing Co. (Chicago, 1898)

[JE 54.535 n465.]

—— *28. Heysinger, I. W., *The Light of China: The Tao Teh King of Lao Tsze, 604-504 B.C.*, Research Publishing Co. (Philadelphia, 1903)

[JE 54.535 n465.]

IV. BUDDHISM (NOS. 29-32)

(In this section, only those works are listed which deal with Buddhism in China, or are based primarily on Chinese sources; other works on Buddhism in general are omitted.)

—— *29. Julien, Stanislas, *Les Avâdanas et Apologues indiens inconnus jusqu'à ce jour suivis de fables, de poésies et de nouvelles chinoises*, 3 vols., Benjamin Duprat (Paris, 1859)

[The first half of this work is a translation from a Chinese Buddhist work; the second half translates various pieces of non-Buddhist Chinese literature. Hence it could equally well have been classified under sect. 1 above.]

1887 30. Beal, Samuel, *The Romantic Legend of Sakya Buddha: from the Chinese-Sanskrit*, Trübner & Co. (London, 1875)

[JE 63.398.]

1888 31. Beal, Samuel, *A Catena of Buddhist Scriptures from the Chinese*, Trübner & Co. (London, 1871)

[JE 63.398 n 4; 86.118, 120 n4. The JE editors cite it as Beal, *An Outline of Buddhism from Chinese Sources*, Trübner & Co. (London, 1870), but apparently no book of this title and date exists, so that it must almost surely be a mistake for Beal's well known *Catena of Buddhist Scriptures from the Chinese*.]

—— *32. Hearn, Lafcadio, *Gleanings in Buddha-Fields, Studies of Hand and Soul in the Far East*, Houghton Mifflin (Boston & New York, 1897)

[This deals primarily with Japanese Buddhism, which, however, is based largely on Chinese Buddhism.]

V. UNCERTAIN ITEMS (NOS. 33-39)

1893 33. Chalmers, John, *The Origin of the Chinese: An Attempt to Trace the Connection of the Chinese with Western Nations in Their Religion, Superstitions, Arts, Language and Traditions*, Hongkong, 1866

[*Stasov*, pp. 102-106, states that V. V. Stasov offered to send Tolstoy a review of this book, in which, however, the book was adversely criticised. Therefore it is improbable that Tolstoy actually read the book himself.]

1893 34. Balfour, Frederic Henry, *Taoist Texts, Ethical, Political and Speculative*, Trübner & Co. (London, 1881)

[*Stasov*, pp. 102-106, 109, 112. It is improbable that Tolstoy actually saw this work, since our source states that on requesting it from V. V. Stasov, Tolstoy was informed by the latter that it was unobtainable.]

1893 35. Rémusat, Jean Pierre Abel, *Mémoire sur la vie et les opinions de Lao-Tseu*, Paris, 1823
[*Stasov*, pp. 102-106. This work is mentioned in a letter of Stasov to Tolstoy, but whether or not Tolstoy was personally acquainted with it is uncertain.]

1893 36. Plaenckner, Reinhold von, *Lao-Tse Tao-Te-king, der Weg zur Tugend*, F. A. Brockhaus (Leipzig, 1870)
[*Stasov*, pp. 102-106. Same comment as on item 35.]

1893 37. Konishi, D. P., *Velikaya Nauka Konfutsiya* (The Great Learning of Confucius), in *Voprosy Filosofii i Psikhologii* (Problems of Philosophy and Psychology), January, 1893, pp. 25-40
[JE 54.436 n150. The JE editors mention this item in conjunction with Konishi's translation of the *Doctrine of the Mean* (item 13 above), but do not state whether it, like the latter, was actually seen by Tolstoy.]

1900 38. Rémusat, Jean Pierre Abel (1788-1832), and
1900 39. Schott, Wilhelm (1807-89): "translations of the works of Confucius and his followers"
[JE 54.448 n181. The JE editors state, without further specification, that such "translations" by Rémusat and Schott were supplied to Tolstoy in 1900 by the Rumyantzeff Museum in Moscow. Various writings on Confucianism are to be found in Rémusat's *Mélanges asiatiques*, 2 vols., Dondey-Dupré (Paris, 1825-26), *Nouveaux mélanges asiatiques*, 2 vols., Schubart & Heideloff (Paris, 1829), and *Mélanges posthumes d'histoire et de littérature orientales*, Imprimerie Royale (Paris, 1843). A translation of the *Confucian Analects* appears in Schott's *Werke des tschinesischen Weisen Kung-fu-dsü und seiner Schüler*, pt. 1, *Lun-Yü* (Halle, 1826).]

BIBLIOGRAPHY

THIS includes only those sources found to be of greatest value in preparing this study, or that deal specifically with Tolstoy's attitude toward Asia. In particular, it does not include the publications which Tolstoy himself read on China (for which see Appendix B), or his own writings and sponsored publications on China (for which see beginning of ch. 3). For a much more detailed bibliography on Tolstoy in general, see Ernest J. Simmons, *Leo Tolstoy* (item 5 below).

ABBREVIATIONS

Biryukov P. I. Biryukov, *Tolstoi und der Orient* (item 6 below)

Gusev N. N. Gusev, *Letopis zhizni i tvorchestva L. N. Tolstovo* (item 4 below)

JE Jubilee Edition of Tolstoy's works (item 1 below)

Stasov *Lyov Tolstoi i V. V. Stasov. Perepiska, 1878-1906*, edited by V. D. Komarova and B. L. Modzalevski (item 3 below)

W *Complete Works of Count Tolstoy*, translated and edited by Leo Wiener (item 2 below)

WORKS AND CORRESPONDENCE OF TOLSTOY

1. Tolstoy, L. N., *Polnoye sobraniye sochineni* (Complete Collection of Works), V. G. Chertkov, general editor, Yubileinoye Izdaniye (Jubilee Edition), Moscow-Leningrad, 1928-

   [Abbreviated as JE. This definitive edition contains a wealth of hitherto unpublished material, accompanied by detailed notes, and is by far the most important source used for the present study. Of the approximately 95 vols. planned for eventual publication, 39 have already appeared (vols. 1-13, 17-20, 25-27, 32-33, 36, 38, 43-44, 46-47, 54-56, 58-59, 63, 72, 83, 85-87). Though future volumes will no doubt broaden our knowledge of Tolstoy's attitude toward China, they will probably not markedly change its major outlines. This is because it is precisely the volumes that have already appeared that contain the largest proportion of Tolstoy's hitherto unpublished writings (diaries, notebooks, letters, etc.) in which his attitude toward China most conspicuously appears; their extensive footnotes, furthermore, provide abundant cross references to similar unpublished material destined for future volumes.]

2. Tolstoy, L. N., *The Complete Works of Count Tolstoy*, translated from the Russian and edited by Leo Wiener, 24 vols., Estes (Boston, 1904-05)

   [Abbreviated as W. This, used in conjunction with the Jubilee Edition, makes the great bulk of Tolstoy's writings readily accessible. It has some valuable items not found in the other standard English translation of Tolstoy: *Tolstoy Centenary Edition*, translated by Louise and Aylmer Maude, 21 vols., Oxford University Press (London, 1928-37).]

3. *Lyov Tolstoi i V. V. Stasov. Perepiska, 1878-1906* (Leo Tolstoy and V. V. Stasov. Correspondence, 1878-1906), edited by V. D. Komarova and B. L. Modzalevski, Izdaniye Priboi (Leningrad, 1929)

   [Abbreviated as *Stasov.*]

CHRONOLOGIES AND BIOGRAPHIES OF TOLSTOY

4. Gusev, N. N., *Letopis zhizni i tvorchestva L. N. Tolstovo* (Chronicle of Life and Works of L. N. Tolstoy), Academia (Moscow-Leningrad, 1936)

   [Abbreviated as Gusev. A concise day-by-day documented chronology, invaluable as a guide for further research on any topic.]

5. Simmons, Ernest J., *Leo Tolstoy*, Little, Brown & Co. (Boston, 1946)

   [The latest biography, making extensive use of the Jubilee Edition of Tolstoy's works. It is published in an ordinary and in a Special Limited Edition; the latter (used for the present study) is documented and contains a valuable bibliography.]

TOLSTOY AND ASIA

6. Birukoff, Paul [Biryukov, P. I.], *Tolstoi und der Orient, Briefe und sonstige Zeugnisse über Tolstois Beziehungen zu den Vertretern orientalischer Religionen*, Rotapfel-Verlag (Zürich & Leipzig, 1925)

   [Abbreviated as Biryukov.]

7. Rolland, Romain, "La réponse de l'Asie à Tolstoy," *Europe, Revue Mensuelle*, Paris, no. 67 (July 15, 1928), pp. 338-360

8. Shahani, Ranjee G., "Hinduism in Tolstoy," *Asiatic Review*, London, n.s. vol. 28 (October 1932), pp. 664-669
   [For an evaluation of these three studies, see end of ch. 1. For a possibly forthcoming Russian study on Tolstoy and China, see Appendix A.]

TOLSTOY'S IDEOLOGY

9. Kvitko, David, *A Philosophical Study of Tolstoy*, Columbia University Ph.D. Thesis (New York, 1927)
   [A useful systematic study, though not always documented as precisely as one would wish.]

CHINESE PHILOSOPHY

10. Fung [Feng], Yu-lan, *A History of Chinese Philosophy. Vol. I: The Period of the Philosophers (from the Beginnings to circa 100 B.C.)*, translated from the Chinese by Derk Bodde, with introduction, notes, bibliography and index, Henri Vetch (Peiping, 1937)
    [The best single work on the early history of Chinese philosophy; useful in the present study for evaluating Tolstoy's understanding of Chinese thought.]

SINO-WESTERN CULTURAL CONTACTS

11. Reichwein, Adolph, *China and Europe*, translated from the German by J. C. Powell, Alfred Knopf (New York, 1925)
    [There is a large literature on this subject. This is the work that happens to be cited most frequently in the present study. Its first chapter contains some brief remarks on Tolstoy.]

BIBLIOGRAPHIES ON CHINA

12. Cordier, Henri, *Bibliotheca Sinica, Dictionnaire bibliographique des ouvrages relatifs à l'Empire chinois*, 2nd ed., 4 vols. plus 1 suppl. vol., E. Leroux (Paris, 1904-08, 1924)

13. Skachkov, P. E., *Bibliografiya Kitaya; sistematicheski ukazatel knig i zhurnalnykh statei o Kitaye na russkom yasyke, 1730-1930* (Bibliography of China; A Systematic Index of Books and Journal Articles on China in the Russian Language, 1730-1930), Gosudarstvennoye Sotsialno-Ekonomicheskoye Izdatelstvo (Moscow-Leningrad, 1932)

[These bibliographies have been invaluable for precise and complete identification of the publications on China read by Tolstoy (see Appendix B) and his own writings and sponsored publications on China (see ch. 3), the citations of which in the Jubilee Edition, Biryukov's *Tolstoi und der Orient*, and other sources, are often inexact or incomplete.]

INDEX

For Tolstoy's relationship with many of the persons, concepts, philosophies, etc., here listed (Confucianism, Lao Tzu, Meadows, etc.), see under Tolstoy.